D1190532

Defining Moments

MY JOURNEY
BACK TO GOD

DENISE WARD

ISBN 978-1-64458-827-7 (paperback)
ISBN 978-1-64458-828-4 (digital)

Copyright © 2019 by Denise Ward

All rights reserved. No part of this publication may be reproduced, distributed, or transmitted in any form or by any means, including photocopying, recording, or other electronic or mechanical methods without the prior written permission of the publisher. For permission requests, solicit the publisher via the address below.

Christian Faith Publishing, Inc.
832 Park Avenue
Meadville, PA 16335
www.christianfaithpublishing.com

Printed in the United States of America

This book is dedicated to Gavin from whom,
in life and in death, I learned far more than I ever taught him.
And to Rhys. My reason for breathing.

Contents

Foreword

There are many times in our lives when we have questioned why something has happened. After the initial shock has worn off and despair sets in, we come to a crossroad for a time being. We choose to either search deeper within ourselves and come to new realizations or we block off thoughts of the event and push them further into our memories.

In her memoir, Denise did what many of us do not have the courage to do… She chose to go deep within herself and search her soul for answers and comfort. During a tragic time in her life, she moved through the grief process with great transparency as she opened up to others sharing her deepest pain. She takes us back through time, allowing us to see in the windows of her heart. Her fortitude while discovering herself was extraordinary.

It is not just her processing of grief that is filled with emotion and examination; it is her spiritual journey as well. Denise takes us back to her earliest memories of her experiences in the church. As her journey unfolds, she finds her way back to God and realizes He never left. He was patiently waiting to have a relationship with her, and when she was at the lowest point in her life, she turned toward Him and found comfort and peace.

Andrea Groubert

Preface

What started out as a journal entry one day to help me try to start working some things out quickly became a short story and has snowballed into a book. The funny thing is that I have never really cared for writing, which is ironic for someone who taught high school English. In fact, as a student, I always made it a policy to avoid writing as much as possible. I put writing right up there with going to the assistant principal's office; I saw it as a punishment. But recently, it has become a method by which I can pull random, chaotic thoughts out of my head, put them down on paper, and organize them to help make some sort of sense from the twisted jungle in my mind. The following is a result of that process.

I, in no way, claim to be any different from millions of others who have struggled with their spirituality, or lack thereof. I simply found writing to be a cathartic process during the most grievous time of my life, a sort of therapy if you will. I also don't claim to be a profound or talented writer, but I do feel a certain sense of obligation to share my journey with others who may still be sitting the fence of their spirituality.

And, also like millions of others, I have no clue whatsoever as to what God has in store for me. But you know what? I don't really care anymore. I trust Him completely and am now happily resigned to submit to His plan for me. I spent too many years ignoring Him for whatever reason, too many years denying Him. I'm done ignoring and denying; I'm done running. I sometimes feel like an old television antenna that needs to be turned from time to time to tune to a particular channel. But now that I am open to letting God into my heart, I find that I need to turn the dial less often. I don't know that

I will ever get to go digital; I don't think anyone ever does. We always need some sort of tuning once in a while. But I hear Him, and I feel Him in so many ways. More importantly, I know that He hears and feels me. He knows that I am His.

Mini Formative Moments

It has always been interesting to me how moments in our lives appear to us at the time they occur compared to how we view them later at different stages (or should I say ages?). As we grow older and experience the ups and downs of life, our perspective most certainly does change, and we realize that what was the worst thing to ever happen to us then is nothing compared to what we sometimes face now in real life. The converse is true as well: things that we didn't think much of at the time, when recollected later, can be significant in regard to the development of who we become as adults.

I also find it fascinating as to how these moments are perceived by others. Because we each have our own viewpoint, what I may see as a defining moment in my life, others may look at and wonder what the big deal is. When I reflect on some of my moments, I can't always draw a direct correlation as to why a particular event affected me the way it did. There are many categories of defining moments in people's lives. Some affect the way we react to particular situations while others dictate how we treat others. What follows are the defining moments that shaped my spiritual struggle and how I came full circle.

As I look back on the events of my life, I realize that there wasn't one single event or reason that caused me to break up with God. It didn't happen overnight; it was a long process that evolved over many years and culminated shortly after my grandmother's death in 1991. And at no time did it ever occur to me that I was moving away from my faith. Even if it had occurred to me, I don't know that I would have done anything to stop it anyway.

Until that era, I had never really questioned God's existence or His role in my own life; I believed as I was told to believe, and I was happy with that. It worked for me. But as I got older, I started to notice too many inconsistencies and incongruities in what I was being taught and what I was seeing. The hypocrisy I was witnessing at the time began to utterly disgust me. In retrospect, although I can't identify the exact moment that I said I had had enough, there are several things that stand out that I call my mini defining moments. These defining moments were not traumatic nor earth-shattering by any means, but they left a stain on my soul somehow and helped to shape me spiritually. I'm not saying I was right or wrong in my evaluation of each situation; I'm simply saying that for whatever reason, my interpretations of the following scenarios had a determinative consequence.

As I look back on the situation now, I am reminded that every person has a story. All too often, we are caught up in our own stories so much that we forget that others have similar or worse struggles. We can never underestimate the impact that some events have on people, nor can we discount their perspectives.

Defining Moment #1

My parents split up in 1968 when I was only three. I don't really remember much about the actual split except one day my dad was there and the next he wasn't. I got to visit him every other weekend, and that seemed to work at the time. I could drone on about how traumatic a divorce can be on children, but to be honest, I never gave it that much thought throughout my earlier life. It was my reality; I accepted it and moved on. It wasn't until I was an adult that I realized just how screwed up I really was, especially as a kid and into my twenties. That was no great epiphany, mind you; I always knew that I was screwed up. I just didn't really know or care why. I'm not blaming my parents for that. I have a feeling I would've been a mess either way.

My parents' divorce wasn't so much a defining moment for me at the time as what came after. My earliest recollection of feeling a sense of vexation toward God was about four or five years after my dad remarried. It suddenly occurred to me that he no longer went to the same church as the rest of his family. He was Catholic. My grandparents were Catholic. That whole side of my family was Catholic. Why then wasn't my dad anymore? I posed this question to my grandmother, and she very casually explained to me that once my dad got remarried, he was no longer allowed to be Catholic because he didn't get an annulment. As I understood it at the time, he had two choices: go to another denomination or get an annulment. The annulment would have basically said that his marriage to my mom never existed. So if he wasn't allowed to be Catholic or his marriage never existed, where did that leave me?

Obviously, as an adult, I can better appreciate the complexities of church doctrine; that doesn't mean that I *agree* with church doctrine however. It simply means that I understand that it's more complicated than I could have imagined then. But as a child whose world revolved around me, it made no sense whatsoever. And if I'm being completely honest, I'm not so sure my concern was for my dad so much as it was for me. Not only was I mad at God, but I was also mad at the whole church. I just didn't get it.

Even though I was baptized Catholic, after my parents' divorce, I was subsequently raised in the Methodist church with my other grandparents where my mother was raised. That was okay with me; I didn't want to go see those mean ol' Catholics anyway. Actually, I shuttled back and forth between several churches. When I was at my dad's for the weekend, I visited his church. Sometimes, even though it was "his weekend," I would stay with my grandparents and go with them to mass. When it was my mom's weekend, I was a Methodist. At least I was getting a look at three very different denominations within the same religion. I just didn't know where I really belonged in all of it.

Defining Moment #2

Perhaps one of the most significant sensations of disgust came at the time of my confirmation, probably when I was twelve or thirteen. I remember our minister having our youth group make this huge green felt banner which was hung behind his pulpit in the main sanctuary. It read,

"Your ♥

+ Your $

= Our Church"

I remember thinking, *Really! You have got to be kidding me!* I found it incredibly tasteless, and believe me, there aren't too many things that junior high kids find tasteless. I wondered if that equation would work with my parents, like "your heart plus your money equal my new stereo." The whole idea was so preposterous to me that I knew I didn't dare try it myself, so what made this minister feel it was okay to pose that to his congregation? I can still feel my own repugnance today. And I am sure I wasn't the only one who was disturbed by this. However, I certainly took note that no one else seemed to be vocal about it, and I was made to feel as though we didn't have the right to call into check the actions of a man of the cloth. The banner continued to hang throughout this man's tenure at our church, and it wasn't until we got a new leader that someone had the sense to take it down. I'm not sure what became of it; perhaps it is used as a prime example at seminary as part of the "stupid things you shouldn't do when you become ordained" lesson.

Regardless, this particular defining moment may not seem like much to most people, but try to look at it from the point of view of an idealistic and somewhat simplistic twelve-year-old mind. This was my introduction into the grown-up world of our church. It set the tone for how my attitude would develop from there. I was left to wonder what I was getting myself into.

Defining Moment #3

When I was in high school, there was this particular woman—I'll call her Mrs. X—who came to church faithfully every Sunday with her two young daughters. They always sat up front by themselves. The forbidden front: or so I thought because no one else ever sat up there, just like being in the classroom where no one wants to be up front by the teacher. There was also this unspoken rule that we all had to sit in the same pews every week for fear of some unknown punishment. Assigned seats if you will. I thought that maybe each of the pew's occupants had to buy it or pay some sort of rental fee. That certainly would have explained why we all automatically went to the same one each week. And it wasn't enough that we had to sit in the same pew; we had to sit in the same *seat* of the same pew, like our reserved seats at the local football games. My uncle (who was only two years older than I) and I had to ask special permission from my grandparents to occasionally go sit in the last row. It wasn't that we were trying to be radicals or buck the system. We just thought it would be less noticeable there if we felt the need to doze off. And I won't even go into what would happen if a new person unwittingly sat in someone else's assigned seat… I'm afraid that could have unleashed a very un-Christianlike throw-down.

What I found disturbing about the X family cannot be attributed to any fault of their own but rather to how the other faithful treated and responded to them. It was evident that Mrs. X and her daughters were very poor; they tried their best to dress up, but somehow, they just didn't compare to the others in their Sunday best. Quite frankly, my friends and I had fervently hoped others might pick up Mrs. X's casual trend so that we wouldn't have to dress up either. No dice.

Ironically, Mrs. X and her girls were probably the most faithful among us. She clearly made a commitment to bring her girls up in the church. They were there for one reason and one reason only: to worship God. Mrs. X always volunteered to help out where and when she could. She had no ulterior motives to feel the power by heading up any committees; she did not feel the need to exchange any juicy tidbits with anyone in the nearby pews, nor did she worry what others thought of her and her girls. I found her to be fascinating in that regard, and I admired her for it.

Over a couple of years, I heard more than just a few snide remarks about how Mrs. X and her girls had the nerve to show up looking like they did. After all, "What would God think?"

I remember saying to myself, "Yeah, what *would* He think? Wouldn't He be thrilled to have them there, and wouldn't He be so ashamed of the rest of us?"

It was so cruel. What's really ironic about this situation is that teenage girls can be some of the snottiest creatures alive, yet we were the ones feeling empathy while the adults set the bad example. Believe me, this little twist wasn't lost on me and my friends. To me, I felt people should just be happy this woman wanted to raise her girls in the church regardless of how they were dressed. And I recall thinking that if that was what it meant to be a good Christian, then I didn't want any part of it.

About twenty years ago, I attended the baptism of my best friend's daughter at my hometown church. Long before this, I had moved to another town, so I wasn't sure if I would see any familiar faces or not. As expected, there were many whom I did not recognize, but two guesses as to whom I saw still sitting up front... yep, Mrs. X.

Defining Moment #4

Toward the end of my high school career, a good friend of mine was dating a girl a few years younger than we were. I didn't know her very well, but at one time, she and her family attended my church when we were younger, and we all went to Sunday school together. Somewhere down the line, her father became a Jehovah's Witness and pulled his family from our church. We did not hear much about this girl after that until Matthew secretly started dating her.

Matthew and I were working together at a local grocery store the day we got the news that "Julie" had committed suicide. Her parents owned an auto repair business outside of town; she took the keys to the garage the night before and turned on a car that was in a bay, placed herself directly underneath the tailpipe, and went to sleep forever. To say the least, Matt was utterly devastated, and I couldn't imagine that such a young girl would come to the conclusion that life was so difficult that she would rather die than be on this earth. These days, sadly, we aren't all too shocked when we hear of someone committing suicide, but back then (very early 1980s), it was virtually unheard of in our little corner of the world, and we were beyond shocked.

Over the next few days, Matt told me story after story about how mistreated this poor girl was based on what I at least considered to be the crazy ideas her father got from his fellow Witnesses. For example, she worked at a pizza shop after school and on weekends. She was forced to sign each paycheck over to her parents as payment for her living expenses, such as her share of the electric bill. When she had to get braces, she had to help pay for them; and when they took a family vacation, Julie had to help pay her own way.

This was all very confusing to us; we had never heard of such a thing. Not that I got everything handed to me; I had to help with my car insurance and other things with the money I earned, and I also had to put some in savings for college. I just couldn't imagine why people would choose to have children then make them pay for things that should be the parents' responsibility. It was outrageous to my teenage mind. I found it very difficult to be courteous to any Jehovah's Witness that came through my line at the grocery store, and we all knew who they were. I hated all of them for what happened to Julie and blamed them all for her death.

The whole time that Julie dated Matt, it was behind her parents' backs. She was not allowed to date, let alone date outside of her church. The fateful straw came when, at the ripe old age of sixteen, her father made arrangements for her to marry an older man from Florida, a man whom she had never met. I remember thinking to myself, *Did we just slip back in time a couple of hundred years?* The whole thing was so creepy to me. It was all so sad to think that while we were all looking forward to things like prom, graduation, and our futures, this beautiful girl dreaded her future so much that she would rather be dead.

And in thinking that, I was left wondering where God was in all of it. Why wasn't her father punished? Why was there no justice for her? Why didn't He help her out of such a horrible situation? It never dawned on me until now that perhaps He did after all.

Defining Moment #5

There was a couple in our church whom I will call Mr. and Mrs. Smith who sat in the same spot in the same pew every Sunday like all the rest of us as if they owned it. Well, actually, *they* probably did own it. Mr. Smith was a wealthy prominent businessman who contributed heavily to the coffers, which would have been wonderful had he and his wife not expected anything in return. However, based on comments from my grandparents and other adults in the church, that didn't appear to be the case. Mr. and Mrs. Smith sat on several important committees within the church, and you can probably imagine how that went for them. It was my impression at the time that they pretty much singlehandedly made all the most crucial decisions, such as who the next minister would be and so on. As I grew up, I supposed that nothing happened in that church without the approval of Mr. and Mrs. Smith.

But all of that wasn't so much a defining moment for me in itself. At that age, I really could have cared less about the politics within our church. I was more concerned about the cute boy whose family had recently joined. Besides, that sort of political jockeying within organizations has probably been going on since the dawn of man. It's what I found out about this righteous couple later that really made an impression on me. As I grew older and came to understand human nature and flaws a little better, I started to hear scuttlebutt in regard to Mr. Smith's roaming eye.

I never was such a prude to think that that sort of thing didn't happen even in the most religious of people, but it galled me that he actually thought he would be above judgment for it. Had he quietly attended church and quietly made his donations, I doubt that so much would have been made of it. But as it was, how could we not gossip about it? He was almost daring us to do so. In retrospect, what made it worse was that we thought we, teens and adults alike, were justified in our gossiping because of who he was.

And personally, I rationalized my own participation with the mere reason that I knew for sure he was straying. As a matter of fact, he was seeing a woman I worked with at the local grocery store, and we all knew it. She made sure we all knew it. I mean, how much gum can one person chew in a week? That's all he ever seemed to buy when he came into the store, so of course, we made our own assumptions before she ever said anything. I was certain his rear end would burn a hole in the pew the Sunday after I found out, and I even caught myself looking that way when we got up to leave just to check. After all, how could he just sit there so pious, so snobbish, making us all think he was more deserving of the kingdom than we were?

I began to consider the idea that perhaps those who felt compelled to proclaim their Christianity the loudest were probably the biggest hypocrites among us. My view of my faith became rather jaded to say the least.

Defining Moment #6

This particular defining moment involves the same family, Mr. and Mrs. Smith's, and it came several years later when I heard second- and third-hand through the small-town grapevine that this righteous couple had disowned their second daughter, "Tina". Tina was a few years ahead of me in high school, and we had lost touch after she graduated. She was just one of those girls that people like to hang around; she was comfortable. She was fun and always in a good mood. I'm sure, in the back of my mind and my friends' minds as well, we always knew she was gay, but we didn't care; she was our friend, and we passed no judgment on her. So given that we were able to see her kindness, loyalty, sense of humor, and overall goodness, you can imagine the immense trouble we all had in understanding how her parents could possibly all of a sudden just pretend she didn't exist.

Of course, now that I myself am a parent, I can, to a very slight extent, understand the letdown they might have felt. I still maintain, however, that your child is your child no matter what. To experience disappointment is one thing, but to exile your own child from the family is quite another. What would happen to us if God exiled us every time we disappointed Him? That would be bad news for me for sure!

But in the name of Christianity (or perhaps more in the name of pride and ego), they turned their backs on their daughter. My friends and I were all mortified, angry, and sad. It wasn't until many years later, after she was diagnosed with a serious health problem that could not be fixed, that I was informed her mother reconciled with her, and they began to mend their relationship, but I'm sure it was never the same. I don't know, however, whether her father ever had anything to do with her before Tina passed away.

To this day, that story continues to be one of the saddest situations I have ever known. When Tina needed her family the most, she found herself virtually alone. The only consolation for those of us who called Tina our friend is that her dad had to live the rest of his days with the knowledge of how he treated his own daughter. Tina was a kind and decent human being who deserved better.

Defining Moment #7

Up until recently, the most defining time of my life without a doubt was watching my Grandma Kate lose her courageous battle with breast cancer. Next to my mom, she was the most influential person in my life, and her death left me in a heap of misery and pain. I have been told on numerous occasions that I remind people of her—not in looks, I look nothing like her, but in spirit and attitude. She could be a bulldog sometimes, and you didn't want to mess with her or one of her own. She could also hold a grudge like nobody's business, to all of which I can totally relate. But she was fiercely loyal to her friends and family and had an incredibly generous heart. If I had to go into battle, I wanted Grandma Kate with me.

When she died, a piece of my soul went with her. I wallowed in my grief, and I was so devastated that I was unable to appreciate her lessons in strength and courage for many years to come.

What my grandma had to endure was unthinkable. Her cancer was inoperable because of a heart valve issue for which she was taking blood thinners, so she essentially became a guinea pig for this new method or that. Keep in mind that this was the late 1980s, and cancer treatments were not even near what they are today (not that today's treatments are all that great). However, she bore her burden with grace and dignity nonetheless, and her faith never once wavered. She knew to whom she belonged and to where she was going, and she was not afraid.

When Grandma passed, I was bombarded with a host of emotions. I have been eternally grateful that I was with her when she finally let go, but I was immediately consumed with anger. Not only was I mad, but I also wanted someone to be held accountable. That someone was God. I wanted to know why He got to take all of the praise, glory, and credit when things went well in our lives but took no responsibility when they didn't. Although incredibly oversimplified and naïve, and most likely to my grandma's chagrin, this was a philosophy to which I clung until recently.

Defining Moment #8

About four months after Grandma Kate passed away, my beloved grandpa began to date. Yes, I realize that was a pretty quick turnaround, but it's not like he had a lot of time to waste. We were all happy for him because we knew this is what Grandma wanted; she did not want him to be alone, and being besieged by family members is not that same as female companionship.

Grandpa John and I were also incredibly close, and we would often talk about his social calendar. He was very active in the local senior center which, all of a sudden, seemed to be filled with nothing but widows. Ladies would just show up out of the blue with a pie, lasagna, or with some sort of other pretense for being at his house. It was funny and a little weird that my grandpa had become the hot new commodity in our little town.

He and I would make mental lists of possible dating candidates and those we were ruling out. It was amazing to note how particular he could afford to be as he was outnumbered about ten to one. He literally had his pick as one of the few eligible men of his age in town. And his reasons for moving individuals from one list to the other were equally amazing to me. Sometimes I had to just shake my head and laugh. But I have to tell you that even as close as we were, I literally just about fell off my chair the day he crossed a line that should never be crossed between grandfather and granddaughter: he brought up sex. And not about *my* sex life, but *his*! I didn't think men his age even had sex any more. I guess I was so used to him being Grandpa that I forgot he was a man, after all.

My grandpa's first lady friend was a longtime family friend who had lost her husband some years earlier. My grandparents had known Betty and her husband for decades. The first time Grandpa decided to invite Betty to church with him, my uncle, his wife, and I all went with them as sort of a show of support. We no sooner parked ourselves in our longtime "assigned" family pew when it began.

I could hear several of what we called the Blue Hairs in the pew behind us quipping about the situation. First, it was clichéd things like, "Kate's hardly dead," or "I bet Kate's rolling over in her grave." Once they beat that horse to death, they began debating the problems that would arise between their religions (Grandpa, a Methodist and Betty, a staunch Lutheran) and that it just would never work. My Uncle Mike and I just rolled our eyes and chuckled. Grandpa had barely begun dating Betty, and these women were already celebrating their eventual divorce! Thank goodness Grandpa and Betty both had their hearing aids turned down.

But once I had time to think later that day, I became upset. How dare they judge him? Why was it any of their business? Were they simply a little jealous because he wasn't courting any of them? And who's to say what the appropriate time of mourning is (especially for someone of his age)? Boy, was I mad, and at that point, I had just about had it. How dare they sit in church, of all places, and question what his family so openly welcomed? I was teetering on that fence of my spirituality already; it wasn't going to take much to push me to the other side.

Defining Moment #9

Grandpa's friend, Betty, was a well-established longtime, reputable businesswoman in our small community. She was the embodiment of grace and dignity. I thought so much of her, which made it all the more crushing when she showed herself to be just as hypocritical as all those in so many of my other "defining moments."

When Betty first started dating my grandpa, I was married to my high school sweetheart. Long story short, we didn't make it. We were too young, and I was way too immature to make a lifelong commitment. Our goals for the future were very different from each other's, and I take equal responsibility for the failure of the marriage. At that time in my life, I very simply and naïvely thought that marriage wasn't all it was cracked up to be and didn't appreciate what it meant to make that kind of promise to another human being. I wanted my way all the time and wasn't willing to make any sort of compromise.

After my dissolution, Betty's grandson, who was a few years younger than me, asked me out on a date. Before the date could actually take place, he all of a sudden cancelled without any explanation. I later found out from his brother that Betty forbade him from dating me because I was a divorcée who liked to visit the local establishments with my friends and drink. It was crushing, not because her grandson was all that great, but because I thought I was a pretty good person and I didn't see anything wrong with my lifestyle. I was completely insulted. The tone in which this all was conveyed was so accusatory and judgmental that I was quite shocked when Satan himself didn't snatch me up right then and there as I stood! After all, according to Betty, I must have been a prime candidate for hell.

A minor hypocrisy in all of this lies in the fact that I met her saintly but potentially corruptible grandson in one of the aforementioned local establishments while he was out drinking with his own friends. And the brother who delivered the condemnation? He worked at one of them. Out of respect for my grandpa, I kept my mouth shut, which is a very difficult thing for me even to this day, and moved on.

That was kind of the last straw for me, spiritually speaking. I felt like I was fighting a losing battle, and I gave up. It was exhausting.

Each one of these defining moments in itself is perhaps no big deal. But in my midtwenty-something mind, these moments became cumulative in their effect upon my position sitting up there on that fence and were powerful forces in determining on which side of said fence I was to find myself. What I now realize, however, is that I was perhaps the biggest hypocrite of all. Here I was judging all of those who were sitting in judgment of others. I was guilty of the very same crimes. Oh, what thirty years can do to a person's perspective!

> *When a defining moment comes along,*
> *you can do one of two things: define the*
> *moment, or let the moment define you.*
> *—Tin Cup[1]*

Chapter 2

The Power of Perception

How does one walk away from God? While my defining moments might not seem like much to most, they were my interpretations of my reality; they were very personal for me for a very long time and obviously had an enormous impact on my life, rightly so or not. These moments were the memorable causes of my breakup with God, and I was holding a serious grudge. I was mad, and there wasn't any one particular person to be mad at, so I was mad at Him.

Looking back now, I think it was easier to be mad at Him and blame Him because of all my defining moments, there wasn't one that was really in my power to fix. They were beyond my control, and I did not possess the maturity to realize it. They were a source of frustration, and I left them unchecked to fester into a hateful mess as I made rationalizations for my inaction. What I did have control over, however, were my perceptions of those incidents as I now have come to realize. In retrospect, maybe those defining moments weren't supposed to be fixed. Maybe they were supposed to be teaching opportunities, not just for me but for all involved. So as an adult, I now find myself looking back on those moments, trying to interpret the lessons that I was incapable of appreciating at the time.

In the grand scope of things, I have learned through the wisdom of age that it makes not one bit of difference as to what church we are raised in. They all have certain regulations and traditions that make them unable to be a one-size-fits-all religion. Some find comfort in more ritualized services while others are more comfortable with less. I eventually learned that where my dad, and the rest of us for that matter, are eventually going to end up at is not dependent on what churches we attend but rather on our character, compassion, tolerance, capacity to love, and willingness to forgive. What we all need to recognize, however, is that these qualities are not exclusively Christian.

It was unfortunate that the distasteful banner incident was my introduction into the grown-up world of our church. The inaction of the adults caused further disappointment for me as I was counting on them to be the ones to affect change. But it reminds me that we are all so far from being perfect and that even ministers have lapses of judgment and fall prey to their egos. This seemingly small incident wreaked havoc on at least one impressionable mind for years. So it also reminds me that, as adults, we need to pause and reflect on our own actions and consider how they might affect others.

The treatment of Mrs. X's family to this day makes me a little sad and a little shameful. I could have been the bigger person and either sat with Mrs. X and her girls or invited them to sit with us. It probably wouldn't have changed the majority of opinions, but I would have felt better about myself, and maybe, just maybe, the adults would have felt some sort of shame that a kid could look past such prejudices and they couldn't. But that would have required me to leave the comfort zone of my own assigned pew with my family and friends, and that was perhaps too much to ask at that time. In essence though, my inaction was no more excusable than that of the adults.

It is always devastating when a young person dies, but when it is by her own hand, it is even more unfathomable. I have to admit that I have searched and searched for a lesson in Julie's death, and I don't know that I will ever come up with one. She saw one way out, and she took it. Was that part of His plan for her? It's not for me to say, but my consolation is that she is in a place where she is loved every day, a place where she no longer feels pain, a place where she can be a child. A child of God.

Contrary to what some think, I believe that those who commit suicide still get to heaven. I can't think for a minute that the God

I know and love would turn His back on those in such a state. He would wrap them in his loving arms and welcome them home.

Both situations with the Smiths have reminded me that judgment does not rest with us. I know that Mr. Smith had his day of reckoning, and Mrs. Smith's is yet to come, as is mine for that matter. And what I know now that hadn't occurred to me then is that people like the Smiths can think they are fooling everyone else, but they still have to look in the mirror; they still have to live with themselves. They still have to answer to someone higher. We all do.

And what can I say about what my Grandma Kate endured? Cancer is most often so random. I let my grief over her loss turn into anger; that anger smoldered and seethed until it mushroomed out of control. I know, however, there was a purpose for what I witnessed because I finally came to appreciate the lessons she was giving me due to a few of my own adversities. My husband is famous for saying that with adversity we have three choices: we can succumb, maintain, or thrive. Grandma was a shining example of how to thrive in the face of adversity, an example that I have had to recall more than once over the years.

Perhaps one the most difficult lessons for me came from the Blue Hair incident with my grandpa. Being the Type A personality that I am, it is so very hard to remember that I can't control what others perceive about certain situations any more than I can control the weather. When those ladies displayed their disapproval of my grandpa dating so soon, I could have made a scene, but to what end? And why should it have mattered to me so much? I was always more than a little protective of my grandad, but duking it out verbally in the middle of a church service probably wouldn't have gone over very well. And after all, his actions certainly did not need to be defended by his overemotional and overprotective granddaughter. Like my grandma, Grandpa knew who he was; he didn't need anyone else's approval.

Lastly and perhaps most importantly, I learned that sometimes things just work out for the best, and we have to trust God's plan for us. Grandpa's lady friend, Betty, made it clear that she did not think I was good enough for her family. I was so caught up in my own indignation that it never occurred to me that there was more to the story. Sometime after this incident, I heard that Betty's grandson had a serious substance abuse issue and needed to have intervention. As I was going out and drinking a lot at the time, I can easily see now that my lifestyle would only have contributed to his problems. God knew what He was doing after all.

As a woman in my early fifties, I can now see my defining moments in a much different light. But back then, I was too angry, too stubborn, too immature, or too whatever to realize that even though I cannot change how others think and behave, I *can* change how I do. Ultimately, I blamed God. It was all His fault. What I've come to understand at this juncture of my life is that it wasn't really God I was mad at; I was just mad. And I think it was in part because of all the garbage we dump on each other and all the damage we seem to do to each other in the name of our own beliefs. We are all imperfect. We are all hypocrites.

But after all was said and done, around the age of twenty-five, I literally packed my bags and walked away from God. For the next several years, my godless life allowed me to behave in any way I wanted without having to think about the repercussions. I answered to nobody. I thought that was the time of my life, but it didn't take long for me to get to the point where I didn't like myself very much. However, I suppressed those feelings and swept them under the pro-verbial carpet so that I wouldn't have to deal with them. We can never truly hide from ourselves though. Just when we think we have everything under control, and we are able to turn our backs for a minute, all that junk comes out from under the carpet. And if we're not careful, it can sneak up and bite us in the hind end when we least expect it.

For most of my adult life I proudly proclaimed myself to be agnostic (not to be confused with atheist). What does it mean to be agnostic? According to *Merriam-Webster*, an agnostic is one who "is not committed to believing in either the existence or the nonexistence of God,"[2] So basically, I decided that I wasn't sure if there was a God, nor did I care to find out. I just knew I wasn't going to spend my life worrying about it.

Not only did claiming to be agnostic permit me to behave as I wanted, but it also gave me an excuse not to *think* about my relationship with God. It was so much easier to pretend He didn't exist. It also allowed me to not take any responsibility for my own screwups. I'm sure that subconsciously, I was thinking that if I believed in Him, then I would have to confront myself, and that was going to be too much work. As a result, I feel like most of my life has been a series of mediocre endeavors strung together by periods of self-doubt, insecurities, and at times, self-loathing.

All of these negative feelings caused me to be super negative with others. I was especially critical and intolerant of religious people. I hated organized religions and all that I thought they stood for, particularly those who tried to force themselves and their beliefs on me. I feel so sorry for the Jehovah's Witnesses that came pandering at my door! It was their fault that Julie was dead after all. I was beyond rude to them, and my behavior was inexcusable. And although I still don't care to have them show up at my house, I am just a bit more courteous to them when I explain that my faith is very personal to me, and I don't care to discuss it with them.

After my move away from God, I got to the point where the mere mention of any religious aspect made me mad. I became very antireligious and apparently wasn't afraid to offend others to let my views be known. After all, if I had to listen to their beliefs and be respectful, why shouldn't they have to respect mine? Of course, I did not occur to me that *respect* was the operative word. As a teacher in a small predominately Christian community, you can imagine that I might have ruffled more than a few feathers. I didn't mean to really. I'm not the type of person who purposely hurts others' feelings, but I had this self-righteous need to inform them of their erroneous way of thinking.

I eventually took it down a notch and realized we are all entitled to our beliefs; we just don't need to cram them down each other's throats. It does indeed just come down to respect. If you criticize someone's belief system, or lack of one, you might as well go up to him and tell him how ugly his clothes are or how unflattering his hairstyle is. It's so very personal. We make our choices based on what we find appealing and what works best for us. But they are *our* choices. We have to own them, good or bad.

When I married my husband, Mike, in 1995 I started to grow up and soften my hard line a bit more. He was and continues to be an incredibly positive influence on my life. He is my rock. Through his love and support, I began to love myself more and to give myself a break. In 1997, we had our son, Gavin. Wow! If there was ever an argument to believe in God, it's parenthood. I distinctly remember thinking the minute I saw him that there must be a higher power because something that incredible couldn't be a random coincidence. He was the most beautiful thing I had ever seen, and I was madly in love with my son.

Even though my leanings were still agnostic, we had Gavin baptized, and when it came time, we took him to Sunday school regularly even though Mike and I did not attend. My thinking was that our children needed to be raised in a church, any church; I had no preference. I never thought churches were without value after all, especially for children. They just weren't working for me. I felt I would be doing my children a disservice if I did not provide them with some sort of background so they would be able to make their own educated decisions later in life. That's how I was raised: in an agnostic home but one where I was made to go to church regularly. I was also encouraged to attend a variety of denominations with friends and other family members. Unfortunately though, as my love for my son grew over the years, I still made no effort to pursue God. I left things as they were. I can't really say why; I guess it was just easier that way. It never dawned on me that He was waiting patiently for my return.

When Mike and I started planning for our second child, I just could not get pregnant. I felt like we were under the gun as I was already pushing thirty-five. We tried everything, and true to form, guess whom I blamed? You got it: God. I felt like I was being punished somehow. I got pregnant the first time we tried for Gavin—why was it so difficult this time? It must have been God's fault again. Or so I thought.

Eventually, after months of frustrating fertility injections and artificial inseminations, I finally conceived. And after a very difficult and scary pregnancy, I gave birth to my darling daughter, Rhys Kathryn, in 2000. My family was complete. But once again I made no effort to reconcile my relationship with God. Things were working out after all. I had everything I could want, so what did I need Him for?

Mount Union College (now the University of Mount Union) in Alliance, Ohio, hosts nationally known speakers each year, sponsored by the Schooler Lecture Series. My husband, a Mount graduate, and I tried to attend them as often as we could. We heard Jeane Kirkpatrick, *Schindler's List* author Thomas Keneally, Holocaust survivor Leopold Page, David Brinkley, and former Lebanese hostage Terry Anderson. I can't remember what most of them talked about quite frankly. However, I clearly recollect one comment made by Terry Anderson because it hit a little too close to home. He was speaking about how his faith remained intact throughout the entire six years and nine months he was held hostage and how he had come to forgive his captors. I remember thinking, *There is no way in hell I would forgive them.* Then he said (and I'm paraphrasing), "There are those who claim to be agnostic. To me, there's no such thing as being agnostic. Those who claim that are simply too lazy to think about God."

I was incensed! How dare he accuse me of being too lazy to think about it! I spent so much time avoiding the confrontation with myself that when he said it, it was like calling attention to the elephant in the room. I didn't want to hear it, and I made every argument for myself against his statement. But you know what? He was exactly right. Of course, it took me nearly twenty years to realize it. Having a relationship with God isn't all that different than other relationships in our lives. It requires a great deal of effort, thoughtfulness, trust, patience, and communication. None of which I was willing to put in the energy for.

No matter how important or how trivial they are, our beliefs influence our relationships, affect our choices, and shape our lives for better or for worse. Yet for a huge chunk of my life, I put way more effort into worrying about what to wear on any given day or what shade to color my hair next, than I did on my beliefs and my relationship with God.

> *Amiable agnostics will talk cheerfully*
> *about "man's search for God." To me, as I*
> *then was, they might as well have talked*
> *about the mouse's search for the cat."*
>
> —C. S. Lewis[3]

Chapter 3

The C Word

Pre *C*

A more recent and absolutely a major defining moment in my attempts to ignore God came in August 2004 when I was diagnosed with stage III lobular carcinoma. Breast cancer. I think I always knew I would hear that diagnosis at some point in my life, just not at the age of thirty-nine with two young children, not that there's ever a *good* time to hear that news. I had many years to prepare myself for this, but somehow, I shoved it to the back of my mind in denial of the probability.

When I was twenty-three, I had an interductal paploma removed from my right breast. All of my family members held their collective breath for several weeks because my grandmother had only been diagnosed with her breast cancer for about a year and things were not going well. I had no health insurance as I was trying to finish up my senior year of college after taking a couple of years off while working two different waitressing jobs. So on top of worrying about my prospects, I also had to worry about how I was going to pay for everything. I went to my grandmother's surgeon, and thankfully, he did the procedure as an outpatient and charged me a very nominal fee. The hospital and anesthesia charges, however, knocked me for a loop. Fortunately, I was able to make small payments until it was completely paid. At the end of all of it, the pathology came back, and the tumor was benign. We could all breathe again.

The day we got the results though, I remember looking at my mom and saying, "I'm going to get it someday, you know. I just know it."

Of course, being a mother, she went into mom mode and tried her best to reassure me that everything would be okay. But I definitely got the impression that she thought I just might be right. After the doctor discussed all the risk factors, I knew what was ahead. I was so much like my Grandma Kate that it was eerie sometimes. So that's why I knew that if anyone in our family would get breast cancer after her, it would be me.

During the years that followed, I was diligent about my breast health. I did my monthly self-exams and had mammograms every five years (once I got health insurance). Everything was fine until I was about thirty-seven. Without any explanation, I noticed something completely out of the ordinary with my left breast. Because it was so similar to what I had experienced fourteen years earlier, I immediately called my doctor's office.

I explained to the receptionist what was going on and that I needed an appointment and a mammogram. She just gave a snotty chuckle and said, "Honey, why don't we let the doctor decide that."

You know, I have all sorts of buttons that can be pushed for a multitude of reasons, but she hit just about every one of them all at once. I don't know what made me want to argue with her—maybe I was just mad or maybe just for the fun of it, but I very matter-of-factly said, "My name is not Honey, and I know my own body. I'm not an idiot, so don't treat me like one. In fact, I'd match my IQ against yours any day. I've had this before, so just make the damn appointment without adding your personal two cents."

I'm sure that after that tirade, she probably skipped over several earlier openings just to teach me a lesson. That's what I would have done if someone had talked to me like that anyway.

Nobody seemed overly concerned, and they certainly were not in a hurry to get me in anywhere. After jumping through a number of ridiculous hoops though, I finally got a biopsy. Sure enough, that's exactly what it was, a benign intraductal papilloma. Duh.

Two years later though, I wouldn't be so lucky. In a routine annual exam, my doctor told me she felt a small lump in my left breast. She thought it was probably just a calcium deposit near the scar from the previous surgery. So she sent me to the same general surgeon who had since turned the focus of his practice to breast-health issues. He immediately ordered a mammogram, and just as suspected, there was a little calcium deposit near my scar. What he *hadn't* counted on was the spot that showed up on the right breast.

Deep *C*

Dr. Green is a jovial man with an incredible sense of humor. If you were to look up the definition of *down to earth*, you would find all sorts of descriptions that match him perfectly. He just has an uncanny knack for putting his patients at ease, yet he knows how to get serious when necessary. He had his office girls schedule me for biopsies in his office on each breast one week apart. He did the left one first. When I left his office that day, he was very positive and made a point to tell me everything looked great. Sure enough, the pathology was fine. The following week, when he finished the right-side biopsy, he said absolutely nothing. He sent me on my merry way and said he would be in touch. I'd had men tell me that after a first date before, but I had never heard it from a doctor. His silence was not lost on me however. I knew.

As if to confirm my suspicions, his receptionist called me on a Friday to ask me to come in on Monday to go over the whole report. Evidently it was too complicated to tell me over the phone. I might be goofy as all get-out, but as I stated before, I'm no idiot. I knew Dr. Green wanted to get me there to break the bad news face-to-face. So naturally, I went in on Monday prepared for the worst after having the worst weekend ever waiting for the shoe to drop.

Sometime over that very long weekend, I decided I would go by myself. I certainly didn't want my kids with me, and I wasn't even real keen on having my husband there either. I wanted time to digest the news before I shared it with anyone else, which might seem funny to those who know me because I usually can't wait to share news, good or bad. That's how sure I was of what I was going to hear. I will never forget that day: Monday, August 15, 2004. It was about 4:45 when Dr. Green brought me back to talk, and as prepared as I thought I was, hearing the word *cancer* felt like someone punched me right in the face.

I did not cry at first because this wasn't exactly unexpected. But Dr. Green and his nurse just looked at me like I had three eyes and snot coming out of my ears. I thought I should probably cry just to make *them* feel better, but I couldn't make the tears come. My mind started to race as a million things came into play at once. However, the minute I thought about my seven-year-old-son and my not-quite four-year-old daughter, the floodgates opened, and I was only able to focus on them. I wasn't worried about what was going to happen to me so much; I was horrified at the thought of my kids having to grow up without me. Who would my husband find for them to call mom? I didn't want another woman raising my kids.

Then it hit me again: why was I being punished? If there was a God, how could He keep knocking me down like this? What did I do that was so bad? Just because I was agnostic didn't mean I was a bad person. I just didn't get it. I'm sure as you're reading this, you're probably thinking that I am indeed a whiny idiot after all, but that's how my mind worked then. And to be honest, I'm not so sure that my feelings then are not so unusual in those types of circumstances. But it gave me yet one more reason to question God's existence.

Everything happened quickly from that point on. None of my doctors were dragging their feet this time around. True to my form, I couldn't have a simpler form of breast cancer. No, that would be too easy. No, I had to have one of the rarest forms that typically presents on both sides, so radical measures were taken. Within one month of my diagnosis, I had a bilateral mastectomy and began the reconstructive process (which proved incredibly painful) with silicone expander implants. One month from the surgery, I began chemotherapy. While I was in the waiting room at my first treatment, I struck up a conversation with on older woman, Helen, who was being treated for ovarian cancer that had metastasized. At one point, she said to me, "Honey, you poor thing. You're too young to be going through such a thing."

I was sitting there thinking the exact opposite. I remember thinking to myself, *My gosh, these people are so old and frail. How can they handle going through chemo?* Perspective.

About fifteen days after my first treatment, my hair started coming out in handfuls. Every time I looked down on the floor, there was another clump. I asked my husband to get his clippers. All four of us went to the garage, and I let the kids take turns shaving my head. This is always such a hard part of the cancer process, especially for women. I think that's because we allow so much of our identity to be tied to our looks, specifically to our hair. I cried for about five minutes afterward and then never cried about it again. I came to find it incredibly liberating actually (not that I want to do it again anytime soon). I now look at my hair completely different than before; it's not as important as it once was. And if I ever have to go through that again, my hair will be the last of my worries.

I felt fortunate that I only had to have three months of treatments as they were decidedly the worst part of the whole process. I half-jokingly told my husband that if I ever had to have chemo again, he better darn well find the best marijuana grown anywhere for me because I never wanted to feel that sick again. With each treatment, the intensity of sickness lessened. However, the sickness lasted longer each time. I had my last treatment on December 15, 2004 and was still incredibly sick for Christmas. I could even smell the chemicals in my body. I smelled them when I went to the bathroom; I smelled them in my skin and hair. I smelled that smell *all* the time.

Because I had taken a short maternity leave a few years earlier with Rhys and I had to take days off here and there for my son's many illnesses, I hadn't been able to build up a significant bank of days. I had to be very careful not to go over, or else I would have had to take unpaid leave. So even as sick as I was, I had to go to work. At the time, I had a very kind superintendent who offered to let me use the sick days that I would accumulate during that current school year. But I still had to be very frugal in case anything else came up. I only missed one day of school during chemo, and that was after the very first treatment. That whole scenario actually ended up working out best for me. I don't think I would have done as well had I been able to take that whole time off school so that I could lie around the house and wallow in self-pity. I was forced to suck it up and move ahead and get up each day to go do my job. Some days were harder than others, but my job gave me purpose and gave me a reason to look forward to each day. My students were amazing during that time. One of my boys even shaved his head in support. I truly believe all of that helped me fight harder to stay healthy and positive.

The reconstruction took about a year from beginning to end. Up to that point, it was the most traumatic thing in my life, but my husband and I made a pact to keep things as normal as possible for the kids, and I think we were reasonably successful at that. We explained everything on their level and answered any questions they had. I realized we might have explained too much though, when one day I got a call from Gavin's second grade teacher about him drawing breasts on all his papers. They weren't just typical doodles of breasts; they were of the insides of them, similar to the pictures we had shown him. He wanted to know all about what was being removed, so my doctor gave me some charts to show Gavin. At any other time in my life, I might have been embarrassed and upset, but this time, I was actually a little proud. At least he was listening, and his doodles were anatomically correct. In fact, they were quite good for being all of seven. I don't think his teacher saw much of the humor in this however.

Throughout the whole *C* experience, I found an inner strength and resolve that I didn't know was there. My husband and I came up with the motto "Now what?" In other words, we have been dealt this hand, and now what do we do? How do we move forward in a positive way? I did not want people to feel sorry for me but simply understand that I might not feel well from time to time. I quickly resolved that I wasn't going to die from this, that it was simply an inconvenience in my life. We would deal with it and move on. I didn't want cancer to define who I was a person; I wanted to be defined by how I *handled* having cancer. I think I did okay.

I'm not exactly sure what happened to me spiritually during that time. I think I must have been substantially numb because I didn't really feel much one way or the other. I do remember the day of the surgery asking God, if there was one, to see me through the whole ordeal. What's sad, though, is that when I actually was through the worst of it, I still didn't make the connection.

As I approached my five-year mark, however, I was probably closer than ever before to analyzing my spiritual position. I stood motionless at the fork in the road for so many years, sometimes leaning more toward one path, then leaning more to the other. But there was something about that all-important benchmark that made me think there might be someone higher to whom I owed a great deal of gratitude after all.

Believe it or not, so many positive things came out of the *C* phase of my life. For example, my plastic surgeon told me I would have perky boobs until I was old and wrinkly. That sold me. I also had a totally renewed appreciation of my family and friends. I had an unbelievable support system that carried my burden with me. My parents, grandparents, aunts, uncles, and cousins all supported me immensely one way or another. And I would be completely remiss if I did not mention my coworkers and friends, especially Kathy. She is an amazing woman whom I don't tell often enough how much I value her friendship and how much I love her.

Post *C*

A couple of years after I was done with my reconstruction, I began doing a few speaking engagements, such as in a Rotary Club, a local AARP chapter, Relay for Life, and even an historical society. Dr. Green gave me several rather large visuals to use at my engagements. My first talk was at a Rotary Club meeting of which about a quarter or more of their members were doctors. When I showed up with them at Rotary, one of the men in charge asked me not to use the charts because they were too visual and also asked me to be very delicate when referring to my breasts. I was stunned! What was I there for? These were well-educated grown men and women after all. If I had gone through cancer of the foot, would I not be allowed to show anatomically correct posters of feet? I felt like I should be ashamed because I had breast cancer. Maybe that is why there are still so many women dying from it; they don't feel comfortable talking about their breasts, especially to men.

When I told Dr. Green about that situation, he just chuckled and said, "Welcome to my world." I thanked him for the visual aids and told him that my other speaking gigs went very well, and they weren't at all offended at my use of the word *breast*. When I offered to return the charts, he told me to hang on to them in case I was asked to speak again. He told me he had a feeling that he would be calling on me one day to help him out. At the time, I don't think either one of us could have guessed it would be for a personal situation.

Several years after that, I got a call from Dr. Green, and he reminded me of my promise to help him out. Without even asking with what, I said of course I would. His wife had just been diagnosed with breast cancer, and he thought I would be of some comfort for her, so he made arrangements for us to talk.

When Mrs. Green called me, she was at the beginning of her cancer journey, so naturally, she was terrified. I was flattered that she would want to speak with me, especially given that her husband was a very talented surgeon who just happened to specialize in breast care. We spent a long time talking about the whole process that I underwent, but I can't really remember many of the specifics. But the one thing I do remember is her remarkable faith. I remember telling her how scared I was initially and that I was agnostic, so I didn't have faith to fall back on. She was very kind but let me know in no uncertain terms that she did have her faith to rely on. My proclamation at that time did not seem out of place, nor was it uncomfortable for me. After all, I had just beaten cancer, and I did it without God.

Or did I really do it without Him? As I reflect on that now, I have to wonder how different my situation would have been if I had leaned on Him. Yes, I was strong, and I did my best to muddle through, but how much stronger could I have been if I would have allowed Him to go through it with me?

Never be ashamed of a scar. It simply means you
were stronger than whatever tried to hurt you.
—Unknown

My Damaged Soul

As I was writing this book, it occurred to me that as humans, we have this uncanny knack of complicating things that should be so simple. For me, that muddling meant twenty years of my life without God, twenty years that I will never get to make up, twenty years of doubt. So after so many years, you might wonder what it is that has me literally running back to Him after I made the declaration over and over again that He probably didn't exist.

It's quite simple. On August 3, 2009, a day after my husband's birthday, part of my soul was ripped out of me forever when my beloved twelve-year-old son died of an asthma attack. We've all experienced loss at some point in our lives, whether it be a relative or a friend. How we react to that loss varies according to the situation. Loss is loss, but some losses are more devastating than others. For example, when my great-grandfather, whom I absolutely adored, passed away from prostate cancer, I was, of course, crushed. But part of me was also thankful that he was no longer suffering. He had lived an incredibly full life, and his time had come. As it's been said, that's the natural order. I experienced similar losses in succession, each one as painful as the one before. However, none of those losses could have possibly prepared me for the loss of my child.

It was the first day of seventh grade football practice, something Gavin had looked forward to all summer. My husband, Mike, a longtime high school football coach, was going to be a volunteer on Gavin's team. It was a particularly hot week, being the beginning of August, but practice was thankfully in the evening. Both of us being

coaches, Mike and I made sure that Gavin was properly hydrating in preparation for the upcoming week. I will never forget how excited he was that day. He couldn't wait to leave. As he and Mike were heading down the steps into the garage, I handed him a gallon jug of water I had frozen for him and wished him a good practice. He stepped back up to the threshold with the biggest smile on his face and gave me a great big bear hug. He always gave the greatest hugs! That was the last time I ever got to see that wonderful smile and hold my son in my arms.

Gavin struggled with allergies and asthma his entire life, but we thought we had been through the worst, and it was under control. I can't even begin to count how many flying trips we made to the emergency room in his twelve short years. But we always made it there. They were always able to restore his normal breathing. Not this time. What was so different this time? We may never know. Our family doctor called it a perfect storm. He said that if ten conditions had to be present to cause his death, then they were all present that day.

He struggled a little during practice but no more than any other time. His asthma was not considered exercised-induced; he would have these episodes sitting on the couch doing nothing but watching television. At practice, he drank his water and hit his inhaler, but his airways wouldn't open up enough to give him any relief. After practice, he told Mike he was having a really hard time, so they got in the car to head to the hospital. We always carried a portable nebulizer with us that plugged into the car, so he got it fired up and off they went. As Mike started out the back drive behind the school, Gavin said, "Dad, I'm really struggling here."

His dad reassured him, saying, "Hang in there, Gavman. I'll get you there. Don't worry."

He no sooner said that when Gavin's eyes rolled back. He slumped in the seat and was gone before Mike could stop the car.

Mike pulled him out onto the front parking lot of the school and started CPR immediately. He yelled for help and two moms, one of whom happened to be a nurse, came to help. One of them retrieved an AED (automated external defibrillator) unit from the school, but it didn't have any effect. Just like that, my son was dead.

And the whole time that was going on, I was at home with my daughter, totally oblivious that my world as I knew it was gone. Mike and the two women desperately continued to work on him until the ambulance arrived and the EMTs took over. My husband's lips were so swollen, cut, and bruised for many days afterward, reminders of his failed efforts because Gavin had recently gotten braces.

I will not forget that phone call that night for as long as I live. It was after 8:30 and I was already beginning to wonder where Mike and Gavin were. Practice was supposed to be over by 8:00, which meant they should be home around 8:15 or so. As soon as I put my ear up to the phone, I could hear the siren of the ambulance. I've never heard my husband sound so scared as he told me through his tears and screams to meet them at the hospital because Gavin had quit breathing. In all the years that we had been dealing with his asthma, we had never once had to call an ambulance. We were always able to get him to the ER ourselves. I immediately went into panic mode as I yelled for my daughter to get her shoes on and meet me in the car. What was really only about a six- or seven-minute drive seemed like an hour as Rhys and I made our way across town.

I couldn't even think straight. I was convinced that Gavin would eventually be okay, but something inexplicable was still gnawing at me. I never imagined that he would die. I don't know what on earth made me say it, but I looked in the rearview mirror and said, "Rhys, please say a prayer for Gavin. Ask God to make him okay."

I clearly knew that this trip to the ER was different from all the others; something was *really* wrong. I called my mom to let her know what was going on and that she should probably head up. She lives about thirty minutes away.

While I was signing in at the emergency room, the intake receptionist got a call. It must have been either from the ambulance itself or from someone in the back. I heard her say, "Oh no. Oh my god. Okay," as she looked up right at me then quickly looked away.

Did I know at that point? I think maybe I did. I'm not sure that I thought he was dead, but I remember feeling that he must be seriously bad off. The receptionist told me that Rhys and I could go back through the doors to wait for the ambulance. When we got to the small waiting area, I again told Rhys to pray for her brother. I, however, did not pray. As I reflect on that night, to this day, I can't say why I did not pray myself, nor why I told her to do so.

I heard the ambulance pull up to the hospital, so I went outside to meet it. As the back doors flew open and my husband stepped out, I saw the look of sheer terror on his face. I heard him screaming for Gavin to please breathe, begging, pleading, cursing. As they were lifting him out, I looked at one of the EMTs as she climbed out as well, and she had tears streaming down her face. It was all so surreal. *Could this really be happening? No, he'll come out of it. He always has before.* I kept telling myself that he would be okay.

Initially, they would only let Mike in the trauma room with him as the doctors and nurses worked to revive him. I thought to myself, *You have got to be kidding me. My son could be dying, and they actually think they can keep me out?* Clearly, they did not realize with whom they were dealing! I kept trying to make my way back through the doors, begging for each staff member to let me back to see my son. Finally, someone realized what was happening as I was pushing my way past several nurses, and one of them finally told me I could come back. I couldn't have been with him more than a minute when I heard a doctor say, "Okay. That's it. We've been at this awhile. He's gone. Time?"

Everything after that went in slow motion. I didn't scream, but I wanted to. I looked at that doctor and begged, "Please don't stop! You can't stop!"

As I slid down the wall, he just lowered his head and walked out of the room, saying, "I'm sorry" as he passed by.

My son was dead.

I went over to where he was lying and just held him and begged him not to leave me. His skin was already cold. But I didn't care; I couldn't let go of him because if I did, then I would have to accept that he was truly dead. I must have been crying a little too loudly because a nurse asked me to lower my voice. *Really! My son is dead, and you don't want me to disturb anyone else?* Mike and I just stood there and held each other for a while. Then we had to go break the news to Rhys that her big brother was gone. How do you explain to an eight-year-old that she will never see her brother again? She was so young and had no idea what was happening. I had left my poor little girl just sitting there, wondering what was going on.

By the time we got out to the waiting room I had left her in, there were so many other people there: the junior high football coaches, all the varsity coaches, our assistant principal, our principal, our superintendent (Mike and I are both teachers at the same school), our family doctor, and others I can't remember. How did they already know? How did everyone else know before we did? After we told Rhys, I started going through my contacts on my cell phone almost mechanically to get hold of others whom we felt needed to know right away.

Even as we were leaving the hospital several hours later, more and more people started to show up in the parking lot: coworkers, students, players, family, and friends. I was incredibly touched at their response, but I couldn't get a grasp on what had happened enough to express anything to them at the time. Word had shot out through the community instantly.

When we pulled into our drive close to midnight, our front lawn was filled with even more coworkers, family, and neighbors. It is said that good news travels fast; but let me tell you, bad news travels even faster. And for once, I am grateful for that. Having so many people around us who cared was an immense comfort as we were in no shape to be alone that night.

The next four or five days were pretty much like being in a thick haze. It was a totally chaotic time, but what I remember most is the outpouring of support and love from the entire community.

Mike and I had to make a lot of decisions as our minds were whirling. We could not donate Gavin's organs because he was already gone, but we were able to donate his corneas, the skin from his back for burn patients, his leg and arm bones, and connective tissues. The donor bank called me as soon as I got in the door, and I had to spend the next thirty minutes answering all their questions. I was in complete shock, which probably explains how I got through that phone conversation. Several people have commented to us that they could not believe we were able to do that, but to us, it was a no-brainer. *Something* good had to come from this.

The three of us lay in the same bed that night, none of us able to sleep. All we could do was hold each other and cry. The rest of that week was a blur. My brother-in-law, Dave, stayed with us the entire week until after the funeral. What a blessing it was to have him there. The morning after Gavin died, he arranged for sedatives from our family doctor for me. At one point, I had to decide not to take them anymore. I knew I had to feel what was happening, and I had a lot to take care of. I remember getting Gavin's clothes ready to send to the funeral home the next day. I mechanically went to his room and started going through his drawers. Out of the depths of my soul came a cry I never imagined I could cry. I crumpled to the floor of his room and just let it loose. I cried and wailed until I was gasping to breathe. I took ugly crying to a whole new dimension.

I know that the week was full of well-meaning people, but sometimes we say the oddest things when we don't know what else to say. I remember an older woman saying to me, "I know how you feel. I just lost my sister, you know."

I was so mad. I very regrettably snapped back at her, "No, you don't. My son was twelve, just beginning his life. Your sister was ninety-one, at the end of hers. You have no idea what I feel right now."

I'm so sorry that I responded that way; it was terrible of me. I know she meant well. But if truth be told, unless you've ever lost a child, you couldn't possibly know what grieving parents are going through, which is good really. You can only imagine what it must feel like. I never got it until it was me, and I wouldn't want anyone else to experience this unbelievable pain.

After the memorial service was over and all went back to their own lives, we were left there alone. I know we were never far from everyone's thoughts and prayers, but we were alone in the sense that we had to deal with the realization that Gav wasn't coming back. My beautiful baby boy was gone forever. All I have to say about that is thank God we have Rhys to give us a purpose to keep going, or else... In fact, my husband's grief and feelings of guilt of not being able to save him were so profound for a time that I thought I might lose him as well. I didn't know how to move forward.

I can't even begin to convey the agony we were in. It is the absolute worst misery on the face of the earth. Ironically, I had just told my husband the week before Gavin died how much I loved my life. I had two incredible kids, a fabulous husband, a beautiful home, and a fulfilling job. What else was there? I didn't think that I would ever again be able to say that I loved my life. How could I? Part of my life is gone, leaving my soul permanently damaged and scarred.

Through the ministry of my friend Andrea, the barriers that I had put between God and me began to tumble down. She and her husband provided so much comfort and guidance that I could write a whole other book about them. Their horses also became an incredible part of my therapy as riding was something that Gavin and I liked to do together. Although my move away from God spread over many years, my return to Him happened in a few short weeks. I just couldn't ignore Him anymore. As I struggled to climb out of the ruins of my life, it was clearly evident that I could no longer do it by myself, nor could I pretend He didn't exist. I was exhausted and emotionally drained. I didn't have the energy or will to fight it anymore. I had to find a way to reconcile my spiritual conflict with my reality.

Gavin's death forced me to do some deep searching in what remained of my soul. This search once again brought me to a proverbial crossroads. Initially, my choices at the crossroads weren't simply right, left, or straight ahead; there seemed to be all sorts of paths radiating from my current location. The only path I could for sure cross off as an option was the one that led back from where I came. There just wasn't any going back. Not this time.

The death of my son literally grabbed me by the shoulders, shook me to my core, and dropped me to my knees. It compelled me to examine my life and what I wanted it to mean. His death is, without a doubt, the biggest tragedy of my life, a tragedy from which there is no recovery. But this tragedy is what led me back to God. Oddly, although I did ask God why, I wasn't really mad at Him. I just didn't seem to have any room in my emotional bank for anger. It was so full of sorrow and utter despair that there wasn't room for anything else. I could drive myself crazy trying to figure it all out; over time, I have learned how to put it in His hands so that I can find some peace by reconciling the contention between my heart and my head. There is much comfort knowing that I can lay my burdens on Him.

The answers do not come easily, and they most definitely do not come without many tears and much anguish. And although I know it will be some time before I have my answers, as I continue on my journey, I do know that I will come out in the end as the person I want to be *because* of the search for answers. I did not then, nor do not now, blame God for Gavin's death. Could He have prevented it? I'm sure He could have, but I do not know His reasons for not doing so.

While I was riding in the arena one day, I was talking with Andrea's husband, Mike, and I mentioned this to him. He said, "But who's to say Gavin wasn't supposed to die sooner, and God let you have him a while longer?"

I thought about that for a long time, and it completely made sense. By the time Gavin was three, he had undergone thirteen chest x-rays and had been in anaphylaxis three times due to a peanut allergy. We discovered the hard way that he was also allergic to milk and was sick a lot. What Mike said to me has stuck with me to this day. I believe that there was a reason for God not intervening. There had to be. Mike also pointed out that perhaps Gavin had something bad in store for him later down the road, and God took him when he did to spare him. Who knows? What I *do* know is that Gavin is far better off now; we are the ones who suffer because we miss him so much and can't be with him yet.

Another very complicated thought that has recently come to me is that, what if God took Gavin because He knew that He would get me back because of it? When people face this sort of tragedy, they can go several ways, and some of them aren't good. Did God know that I would return to Him? Gavin was always His, no ifs, ands, or buts. In fact, he told my husband once that he thought anyone who didn't believe in God should have to go to jail. Mike just chuckled and told him that it wasn't all that long ago that that very sort of thing actually happened. But Gavin's faith was so strong that when he appeared at the gates and if God gave him the choice of staying with Him or coming back to us, Gavin would have decidedly said, "I'm staying with You."

So my question is, did God keep Gavin with Him knowing that losing my son would bring me back to Him? I have not voiced this idea until now, but is it really out of the scope of possibilities?

Maybe God is trying to teach me patience because I will have to wait what will seem like an eternity until I meet Him to understand the grand plan. Don't get me wrong—God still has some 'splainin' to do, but I know all will be revealed eventually. Or, maybe there wasn't a grand plan at all. Maybe it was just Gavin's time. I just don't know; that's an awful lot of maybes. I have learned many lessons lately, and life is definitely too short to spend it being mad at God for things I can't possibly expect to understand.

While Mike and I grieve together, we each have our own burdens to bear as well. He carries so much guilt because he couldn't save Gav, and I'm sure the visions of his son dying in front of him will stay with him forever. But what causes him so much pain brings me enormous comfort and gratitude. Gavin was with the person he loved most in this world when he died. He felt safe. He wasn't alone. He wasn't with strangers. He was with his dad.

I honestly don't know how we have managed to go on from that devastation. There was a time when I thought there was no possible way I could, yet here I am. There were many days when I thought to myself, *I don't want to be here anymore. I'm done.*

Yet each morning, I got up and went on with each new day. I don't know how. Many times I still feel like I'm not needed here anymore. Mike doesn't need me. Rhys doesn't need me; she has her dad. But Gavin needed me and now that he's gone, what's the point? He gave my life purpose. So much of my identity was tied to him that there were times I thought I would to have to reinvent myself if I was going to survive this. But God has a gentle way reminding me from time to time that I most certainly still have purpose here, and her name is Rhys. What kind of life would it be for a young girl to grow up without a mother? She does indeed need me. And I need her.

Those reflections are just the tip of the iceberg of my dark thoughts. But I do feel that through Gavin's death, whether connected or coincidence, I have definitely come running back to God. I have realized that believing in Him and what He has to offer us is the only thing that makes the rest of this life bearable. If I had to live for what may well be many years to come without the idea that I would see my son again, I don't think I could bear it. If I had to live this life with all of its harshness without reaping the rewards of heaven, I'm not sure I would want to be here. But as it is, this awakening in me is slowly lifting the enormous weight from me, and as I learn to feel His light, it brings me unimaginable comfort. And although I will never be whole again, I know that with time, God will ease my pain. He knows that I need to have time to feel Gavin's absence. I know He's with me. I know by the people He has placed in my life, and I know by the strength He gives me to get through each day.

The death of a child is like losing your breath
and never catching it again. It's a forever panic
attack, feeling your heart dying as your soul
is screaming for him and no matter what you
try to do, you continue to lose your mind.
                                        —Unknown

Chapter 5

Signs

Until my son's death, I never really put much stock in signs from beyond. Probably because I am now so desperate for them, I have started paying closer attention. It wasn't until several months after Gavin's death that my husband and I started sharing what we perceived to be signs. I think we kept them to ourselves out of fear that the other would think we were nuts. Once we started to compare notes, we were able to find so much comfort in sharing our experiences. There are many who will disagree with what I perceive as signs either from Gavin or God. That's okay—this isn't their book. And if it turns out that these signs were coincidences, I don't want to know. These signs were what brought me small amounts of joy that had been very hard to come by.

Dreams

Immediately after Gavin's death, I started to plead with God for any little sign He could give me that Gavin was okay. Sounds ridiculous, doesn't it? He was with God after all—how could he *not* be okay? I'm sure that was just a normal mom reaction; all moms worry about their kids being okay. But my need to know became all-consuming.

Two nights after Gavin died, I had a dream of him. I don't often remember my dreams. If I do, it's mostly just after I wake up and just long enough to say, "That was really weird," then forget about it. But this particular dream, as brief as it was, was so clear and vivid, I felt like I could have touched Gavin's face. He was sitting on my father-in-law's lap with his arm around Glenn's shoulders. My father-in-law, whom I truly cherished, passed away in 2001. Gavin had the biggest poop-eating grin (a term I often used to describe his smile) on his face. He wasn't wearing his braces or glasses. He looked so happy to be with his papa again, and he simply said to me, "Mom, I'm okay."

That was it. Nothing elaborate, but just enough to let me know he heard me. I got what I asked for. But why wasn't that enough?

Now, more analytical and skeptical people might say this happened simply because I wanted it to, not that Gavin was actually communicating with me. Perhaps, but I choose to believe it was him, and he was trying to ease some of my pain. However, at the time, because I was so fresh in my grief, I wasn't as confident about that dream as I am now. It wasn't until a few days after this dream that I shared it with my husband. He just looked at me like I had said I was from another planet. Finally, he said, "You're not going to believe this, but I had a similar dream of him that exact same night."

In Mike's dream, Gavin just smiled and said, "I love you, Daddy."

Was this just another coincidence? I no longer think so. Since those early dreams, Mike and I have both encountered too many other incidences that just can't be written off as mere coincidences. I think that God allows our loved ones to watch over us and bring us comfort without revealing directly to us the wonder of heaven.

It was a long time before I had another dream about Gavin. I begged him to come to me again, but just as when he was alive, he ignored me. Then six months after the first dream, I had another visit from my son. In this dream, I was up high and was looking down on him, probably from a balcony at Myrtle Beach, our favorite vacation spot. I saw him on a walkway below, headed to the beach. He had on his favorite black sleeveless t-shirt and a pair of shorts. As soon as I saw him, I started yelling at the top of my lungs to someone inside the condo: "Oh my god! It's Gavin! It's really Gavin! Look! He's back!" Then I yelled down to him, "Gavin! Gavin! Up here! It's Mom!"

He stopped, turned casually, looked right at me, again with his famous smile, and waved to me. Once again, that's all there was to it, but it was enough to carry me through another few weeks and give me reason to smile. Curiously, he seems to know when I really need him the most. I truly believe he is with us always. The comfort that notion brings us is immeasurable.

The week of what would have been his thirteenth birthday came with a lot of pain and what-ifs. My husband and I both teach in a small rural high school that is housed on a K-through-12 campus. Even though we don't live in the district, we moved our children there on open enrollment. Gavin was all set to enter the seventh grade when he died.

Until the week of his birthday, it hadn't really occurred to me just how hard his death continued to be on his classmates. A longtime friend of ours told me that her son, one of Gavin's closest buds, was really struggling and missed him terribly. I had been so wrapped up in my own grief that I nearly forgot about anyone else's. I can't imagine how incomprehensible death must be to kids. If *we* struggle with the concept so much, how can we possibly expect them to get over it so easily?

With that in mind, when I was asked by a friend about what the school could do for us on February 4, I immediately said that we should do something to involve the seventh graders to give them some release. "How about a balloon launch?" My high school principal went right to work: he had the seventh grade language arts teachers make this a class project. The students composed messages to Gavin that were tied to helium-filled balloons. Each class picked a spokesperson to read the message and release the balloon. I thought this was such a fitting way for all of us to pay tribute to Gavin, to let him know that he was still in everyone's hearts. In the process, I hoped the students would feel some peace about the tragedy they were a part of. I felt really good about the way Gavin was remembered by his friends.

The weekend after the launch, Mike told me he had another dream from Gavin the night before his birthday. Mike said, "I don't think he was happy with us."

In the dream, we were all outside around the flagpole: all the seventh graders and staff, some elementary teachers, Mike, Rhys, and

I and my parents. Gavin was looking around at all of us with a very sad, almost angry expression. He stood in one place and just searched our faces, but we couldn't see him. It was almost as though he didn't want all of this as though it was too sad for him to bear.

As soon as I heard this, I got sick to my stomach. I had just recently finished reading a book by Allison DuBois entitled *We Are Their Heaven.*[4] Allison is a well-known medium whose talents and experiences were the basis of the hit show *Medium.* In her book, she states that our loved ones don't like to feel so much sadness revolving around them. They want us to move on and heal because they are in such good hands where they are.

In our attempts to help ourselves and Gavin's friends, I was sure we had somehow hurt his feelings. I immediately went into his room, where we keep his ashes, and asked him to forgive us, to forgive me. And although I did not perceive any signs from him concerning this matter, I know that he forgave me. That was just his nature. He always forgave so many of my shortcomings as a parent. I'm sure there is a lesson in all of that somewhere as well.

It is no coincidence that in the dream Mike had the night before the balloon launch, we were all around the flagpole. That is exactly where the event was held. We did not know until the morning of the launch where we were to go, so how did that fact end up in the dream if it had not been sent by Gavin? Hmmm.

Because of the message Gavin sent us via Mike's dream, I felt he wanted us to start to move on. We knew that the first year would be the hardest, and we had already gotten through some pretty major firsts: Rhys's birthday, Thanksgiving, Christmas, and his birthday. And although we still had a few more firsts to get through, such as Mothers' Day, Fathers' Day, vacation, and the first anniversary of his death, I felt it was time to focus less on the grieving process and start focusing more on healing. Even after all this time, we still have a long way to go, but we're working on it. Even though his birthday was a difficult time, it marked the beginning of a new normal for us mostly because of my husband's dream.

My Grandpa John's birthday was close to Gavin's, so we always celebrated them together with our extended family. Shortly after we had dinner at our place for Grandpa's eighty-eighth birthday, I had yet another Gavin dream that was very different from the others, and it left a lingering sense of something unresolved and unsettling. In this dream, Grandpa and Gavin both came to me with a proposition: we could have Gav back but only until he turned fifteen. At that time, God would take him home again. We had to decide right then and there. Gavin never said a word; he just stood there. Only this time, there was no poop-eating grin. I woke up before I gave my answer, but I had to sit on the edge of the bed for a few minutes before I could get up.

What *would* I do if given that choice? Part of me thought I would take him back in a heartbeat, but the other part thought I couldn't go through the pain again of losing him. Besides, he is way better off where he is. *We* aren't, but he's just fine. If we brought him back, it would be for our own needs, not his. Would that be fair? I felt like God was giving me a test or at the very least something to think deeply about.

In Allison DuBois's book, she emphasizes that our loved ones communicate to us through our dreams because that is when our minds are most open. I am fully aware that many of you reading this right now are thinking that I have completely gone 'round the bend. I get that. There was a time when I would have thought this way myself. I don't anymore. There is an inexplicable feeling about these dreams for me and my husband. They are so very different from the dreams that I occasionally remember. The best analogy I can give is that this difference is akin to 2D versus 3D movies. And if in the end, these dreams do turn out to be nothing more than coincidences and wishful thinking, what harm is there in thinking they are from Gavin now? The peace that most of them brings is worth any possible misinterpretations on our part.

Orbs

In September of that year, about a month after Gavin died, a colleague of mine and my superintendent arranged for me to go to an educational presentation in Phoenix. I had never been that far west, so I jumped at the chance. While I was there, I took a desert trail ride out in Mesa at dusk, which turned out to be a very spiritual experience. I can't explain why, but I feel that I really connected with God out there, and a feeling of peace washed over me. After I got home and developed my pictures, I noticed something strange and inexplicable. While on my desert ride, my guide and I encountered a coyote. My first one ever. He came up to us, about six feet from my horse and just watched us. We stopped and checked him out as he was checking us out. When I looked at the pictures afterward, I was disappointed that they didn't come out very well. In fact, several of my pictures from that night seemed to be messed up. There were these orblike things all over my pictures. A friend explained to me that while most people chalk orbs up to dust particles, many other believe they are of the spiritual world. That certainly sounded good to me and explained, to a certain extent, the spiritual connection I was feeling.

At the time of Gavin's death, my entire family and I were planning a huge five-year cancer-free celebration. We rented a hall, made all kinds of food, had people from all over donating prizes for a Chinese auction and asked everyone to wear pink. We all had a lot of money invested in it, so we didn't want to cancel it. Our plans were to donate the money to the county health department's mammogram project. A friend of mine contacted the hall and got it moved to October. In the pictures from that night, there are all sorts of orbs from a variety of cameras.

I was curious about this and wanted to know more, so I did some research on the topic. Again, while some attribute these orbs to dust or moisture on the lens of the camera, many believe that they are of the spiritual world. I won't try to convince you one way or the other—I know what I think they are. Ironically, none of the pictures I have taken since that party have had orbs in them, even pictures taken with the same camera. I see this as an indication that Gavin is completely at peace.

Man's Best Friend

About three weeks after Gavin died, we finally decided to adopt a dog. Gav always wanted one in the worst way, but because of his allergies and our busy schedule, we just couldn't have one. Gavin was such an animal lover, and he regularly volunteered with me at a local no-kill animal shelter, Alchemy Acres Animal Sanctuary, in Salem, Ohio. We had three cats, but Rhys really wanted a dog, and we hoped that it would be comforting for her.

I spent several hours one day looking at all 120-some dogs available for adoption. I wanted all of them. However, I eventually narrowed my selection down to three. I presented my scouting report to my daughter and husband and informed them that they would have to help make the final decision. As we stood looking at the chosen three, I knew this was going to be agonizing. It was like being at the year's biggest one-day shoe sale at Macy's and only having enough money for one pair. It wasn't a decision we wanted to take lightly. After all, this dog was going to be the newest member of our family, and the fit had to be just right.

Only one of the three contestants was already housebroken, but Rhys thought he was too ugly. Then there were two. I kept trying to find a reason to eliminate one or the other and got nothing. Of course, my husband, who really didn't want a dog period, said it was up to me and Rhys. No help there. I was just about to the point of flipping a coin when something drew me to the white one. Rhys and Mike both agreed.

The day I brought Dingo home, he beat a straight path to Gavin's room as if he had been there before and knew where he was going. He jumped up on the bed and peed on it right in front of my husband. When Mike told me about it, we both just kind of laughed because we were both thinking the same thing: that Gavin sent him to us to help our family heal. Dingo certainly had many of Gavin's traits. He *clearly* had ADHD, but he was also extremely lovable and loyal, just like Gavin.

Also like Gavin, Dingo liked to roam the neighborhood. We used to call Gavin the Mayor of Countryside (the name of our development) because he liked to get out and see people in the neighborhood. We never knew where he might end up. When we first got Dingo, we knew he wasn't going to stay put. Training him was proving more challenging than we anticipated, so we installed an electric boundary and put a shock collar on him. He must've had a girlfriend somewhere because he was willing to take the shock to go gallivant through the yards.

Birds of a Feather

Once Mike and I found out we were having a boy, we wanted to select a unique name that had special meaning. As a tribute to his late mother who came from Wales, we wanted a Welsh name. We each looked through a name book and wrote down our top three choices of Welsh origin, then compared lists. We both picked *Gavin* as our number one choice. It was meant to be. In Welsh, *Gavin* means "white hawk," and over the years, he received various hawk figurines from family members. So hawks had become symbolic of Gavin. He always got such a kick out of the story of his name; it made him feel special to know the connection to his heritage.

In Allison DuBois's book *We Are Their Heaven*, she relates that many times, our deceased loved ones send us signs using birds that have meaning to us. Obviously, the bird that has most meaning to me is a hawk. During the fall after his death, I would go home from school to change quickly then head up to my friend's to go horseback riding. My house is in a development off of a highway bypass for two significant state routes. The road that leads out of my development intersects with the bypass. At the opposite corner from the stop sign, there is a group of several trees in a row that seem so alone and out of place. The tree on the left has clearly been dead for some time; the bark has been picked off little by little over time, and the once-hearty limbs are now merely stubs.

Before Gavin's death, I never paid these trees much attention. But now, for whatever reason, the dead tree seemed to call to me. One day, as I sat at the stop sign, I remember thinking how odd it looked in the group, with the other trees so lively. *Why had this one died while the others thrived? Had it been diseased? Was it starved of vital nutrients? Did it have asthma too? Wait. What!* An incredibly odd idea suddenly struck me that maybe there was a direct parallel between that tree and my Gavin.

Why did my son so suddenly die? He had been doing so well, and his asthma was under control. Or so we thought. Death is sometimes so unbelievably arbitrary. We are offered no explanation, rhyme, or reason. Looking for an explanation can often drive us mad. If a tree expert cut that dead tree down, dissected it, examined it microscopically, ran all sorts of biological and chemical analyses, would he be able to determine its cause of death? And if he did find cause, would he ever know *why?*

Once cause of death was established for my son, many experts tried to figure out why. Unfortunately, until we are called home and stand in front of God, we will never know why Gavin died. Then and only then will we get all of the answers to our questions. *Honk, honk, honk.* Evidently, as I sat contemplating this, I forgot I was at an intersection and that there might be someone else who wanted to get going, so I made my turn and went on my way. But the tree stayed in my thoughts for hours that afternoon.

The next day, I went through the same routine of rushing home to change to go riding without giving my dead tree any thought. However, after I changed and headed down the road again, I remembered the tree that had dominated my thoughts the previous day. I don't know what made me look over at it, but when I did, I saw this beautiful red-tail hawk perched at the top of this tree that now only resembled a pole. He seemed to be looking right at my car. As I drove past the tree, I watched him out of the passenger window, and I swear he watched me.

I was so elated that I almost forgot I was driving a car. I immediately felt a spiritual connection to Gavin. While hawks are not surprising to see in northeast Ohio, I certainly don't think they are overabundant either, especially sitting that close to a busy highway in a residential area. The vision of the magnificent hawk sitting so undaunted on my dead tree stayed with me all afternoon and the next day as well.

This exact same scenario occurred the following two days. I could hardly believe it. Why would this hawk, assuming it was the same one, be on the same tree (in a group with others) for three consecutive days at the same time of day, which by the way, was around 3:00. Anyone see a theme here?

As I headed to my friend Andrea's that third day, just outside of city limits, something utterly bizarre happened, something that still makes me go "hmmm" today. In the middle of my lane was a dead hawk on its back with its feet slightly up in the air. I could not have possibly imagined what that meant. It was most haunting. I have not seen my hawk on my dead tree since, and believe me, I look every single day in hope. I do, however, take special note any time I see one somewhere else. Sometimes I don't see one for weeks, and I find myself asking God to send one to me so that I know Gavin is with me.

Such was the case one winter day several months after I first saw "my" hawk. I had had a terrible day at school not so much because of any one thing. It was just another one of those days that creeps up on me every so often when I find myself really missing my son. Consequently, everything else was affected by my mood. On the way home, as I approached my turn, I started talking out loud to Gavin, a common habit, and I literally begged him to send me a hawk because, boy, did I need one. It's a good thing my daughter rode home with her dad that day, or else she would have really thought her mom had lost it. While making my turn, I looked over to my tree as I had done automatically for months, really expecting to see my hawk. I don't know why I felt so letdown when I didn't. Did I really expect Gavin to deliver? Yeah, I think I actually did.

My bad day wasn't getting any better; that is, until I drove about a quarter mile more. There it was, sitting on a low wire next to the road: a beautiful big robust hawk. Thank goodness no one was behind me, or else it could have been ugly. I sat in the middle of the road for what seemed like a few minutes, just looking at him and bawling. I was so happy. I felt the weight of my day lift entirely.

From that point on, whenever we saw a hawk, we told Rhys that it was Gavin keeping his eye on her. The thought was very comforting for us all, but I think it brought some peace to her, and she realized that the ones we love are never truly gone. They are wherever we are.

Music to My Ears

Shortly before my son's death, he hounded me and hounded me to buy him two new ringtones for his phone. Yes, my twelve-year-old had a cellphone. For those of you who think I'm nuts, let me tell you that (a) I probably am, but (b) he was never too far out of reach. As a reward, I agreed to download his two favorite songs for his incoming texts and his ringtone. His text signal was "No Surprise" by Daughtry and the ringtone was "Second Chance" by Shinedown, both of which I liked as well. Any time either one came on the car radio, we'd crank it up and sing along. Gavin, unlike my daughter, never complained about my singing and seemed to find it funny when the two of us would bust out in song together. That is just one of the many little things I miss doing with him.

At the time when Gavin died, each song had already spent its time on the hit list and wasn't played as frequently anymore. I typically listen to classic rock, but occasionally, out of boredom, I flip through the stations for something different. About two months after losing Gavin, I went through a spell of several weeks of hearing one of those two songs every time I was in the car. Again, where others see this as coincidence, I do not.

This is yet one more way, according to Allison DuBois, that our loved ones attempt to communicate with us: through the radio. Whether or not this is the case isn't the point so much as how I felt each time I heard one of those songs. Earlier in my grieving process, they brought me to tears because I knew I would never again have the opportunity to be goofy with my son like singing in the car together. But during the time I referred to earlier, those few weeks I heard his songs so frequently, I no longer cried when they came on. Instead, I felt a warm and loving connection to Gavin that wasn't accompanied by sadness. In fact, I may have even smiled a time or two while remembering. I was as sure then as I am now that he had a hand in it somehow. Now, when one of his songs comes on, which isn't often at all, I crank it up and sing along just like before even in spite of my daughter's protests.

I am fully aware that there are many people who do not believe in signs from our loved ones, that they can communicate with us, and that's okay. I understand that. But I choose to believe that these signs came from Gavin and are his gifts to me. They always seem to come when I need them the most. And I also choose to believe that not only are they gifts from him but gifts from God as well, for who knows my heart better?

He knows how much I am hurting and suffering still. He knows that once in a while, I just need a little reminder of the love my son and I shared to help get me through a rough day. And although God may not want us to know what heaven is like until we ourselves get there, I choose to believe that He loves me enough to allow Gavin to give me the tiniest pieces of joy and occasional peace.

I can no longer see you with my eyes,
touch you with my hands, but I will
feel you in my heart forever.
—Unknown

Chapter 6

Gifts from God

To say that my son's death completely altered my thinking is the understatement of my life. When he died, for some unknown reason, I quit running from God and found that He was still there, waiting patiently for me. When I needed Him the most, He didn't abandon me as I so deserved. On the contrary, He showed himself to me in so many ways and proclaimed Himself so loudly that I couldn't possibly ignore Him. I slowly learned how to lean on Him and trust Him. After all, He was the one in control, and I had to learn to quit trying to wrestle that control away from Him. Somewhere in all of this, I came to realize that I never really had control in the first place; it was always Him. When I let go of my end of that tug-of-war rope, the healing began.

Although I feel the signs from Gavin ultimately came from God, there are those gifts that come directly from Him. Call them signs, messages, lessons, gifts, or what you will; the bottom line is that I now know they do indeed come from Him. Some of those gifts were lost on me until I opened my heart, and others came through loud and clear from the onset.

One of the things I lament the most is that we never got to see what could have been with our son. Gavin was always what my husband and I affectionately called high maintenance. From the minute he was born, he suffered from innumerable allergies and asthma. In addition, at the ripe old age of four, he was diagnosed with ADHD (attention-deficit hyperactivity disorder). We did not immediately put him on medication because he was just too young. Over the next several years, we watched him struggle in school to the point that we couldn't let it go any longer. His doctor at a renowned children's hospital about an hour away was all about giving him labels but was not too keen on helping us deal with the behaviors. In fact, in each session, he would proudly puff out his chest in an a-ha moment, like he just discovered the cure for cancer, and rattle off some acronymic diagnosis and an explanation that seemed to be in an alien form of communication. Then he would simply suggest this book or that one that might offer us some insight into our troubled son. I was pretty sure that's what we were paying *him* for. He suggested so many books during the time we were with him that my husband and I had to wonder if perhaps he was receiving some sort of commission from the publishers.

Over the next few years, Gavin was also diagnosed with Asperger's, OCD (obsessive-compulsive disorder), ASD (autism spectrum disorder), and ODD (oppositional defiant disorder), and so on in straw-grasping attempts to put some sort of label on him that would stick. Of course, along with each diagnosis came a new medication as well. Most of the time, we were made to feel like idiotic parents who couldn't control their child. We would leave the doctor's office completely baffled every single visit. I would go home to research.

It didn't matter what he was labeled with. We needed to know how to help him so he could be more successful in school and, let's be honest here, make life a little more bearable for all of us. As it turns out, all we really needed was a lot of patience and time. Something that I continue to struggle with is that I spent so much time trying to get him to fit the way everyone else thought he should be that I often missed and failed to appreciate the beauty of the person he was. That is an incredibly heavy burden that I am slowly learning how to give over to God. So many other people as well, including medical and educational professionals, tried to put every label imaginable on Gavin. Still to this day, I am at a loss to come up with any better label than Gavin was just Gavin. No further definition needed, especially to those who knew him. He was truly my greatest gift.

Unfortunately, it took Gavin's death to open my eyes to the first of God's gifts to be explored here. In the spring preceding his death, we were able to take him off all of his ADHD medications. To use a cliché, our son was blossoming, and we finally began to see light at the end of the tunnel. He was maturing into a fine young man. He was always a very loving boy, but now, he was beginning to turn into a man right in front of my eyes. Don't get me wrong though. He still had what I call a junior high mouth, but that's normal and I knew it would pass. Eventually.

I experienced so many proud-mom moments that summer, and we had the best family vacation *ever*. His asthma seemed to be under control. He was healthy and was loving life. Mike and I were really excited about the prospect of starting seventh grade. And for a kid who didn't particularly like school, even *he* was somewhat excited. School was more of a social event for Gavin. In everything he did, if he wasn't having fun, he didn't see the point. We just knew seventh grade was going to be a turning point for him.

It took my friend Andrea to point out to me after his death that maybe God knew Gavin's time was coming to an end and gave us that great summer with him because He knew it would be our last. Boy, I really had to let that one soak in. I was looking at the glass half empty: how tragic it was to lose him just when everything was starting to go so well for him. But as I started to adjust my perspective, I realized that Andrea's point made so much sense. Once I looked at the half-empty glass from another angle (don't get me wrong—it was *still* half empty), the burden on my heart wasn't as great. However, along with that comforting notion came so much guilt at times. Had I known it was his last summer, oh, the things I would have done differently! I have a whole new appreciation for many of our trite sayings in regard to enjoying each day.

In this lesson is another gift from God, and that is the time that I have with my daughter. It's so easy for us as parents to put activities with our kids on the backburner. Our jobs and other commitments often consume us, and time with our children, unfortunately, gets shoved down lower on our list of priorities. Because of God's lesson, it is my goal to enjoy every minute I have with Rhys. She is the other half of my heart.

I think God also gave me another gift in the circumstances under which Gavin died. As horrible as it was, it could have been worse. I know this may come across as odd, but bear with me. I say this because he could have been all alone. Earlier in the day, he went for a bike ride through his "mayordom." He could have had an asthma attack then and died alone. He jumped in the pool for a bit while I was inside the house. He could have had an asthma attack then and died alone. He was watching a movie on the couch while I was upstairs putting laundry away. He could have had an asthma attack then and died alone. From my perspective, his death would have been exponentially worse for me had he died alone. But as I mentioned earlier, Gavin was with his dad. And he had just come off the practice field. He loved football and worshipped his dad. So as odd as it may sound, I find at least some comfort in that. My only hope is that someday my husband can find comfort in this gift as well.

Another gift from God came through a former student of mine who is also the daughter of my friend Nancy. Katy was a music student at a Christian college in the South and was doing her internship with a local Christian recording studio. One day, because she is a fabulous singer, she was asked to warm up the mics for a special guest. She was then invited to sit in on the session with said special guest. As it turns out, this guest was none other than contemporary Christian recording artist Steven Curtis Chapman.

Before he left, Mr. Chapman inquired as to whom he had heard warming up the mics. For doing so, he handed Katy two copies of his then-unreleased CD *Beauty Will Rise*. For those of you who don't know about him, he lost his four-year-old daughter in an incredibly tragic accident about a year prior to the release of this CD. *Beauty Will Rise* is a result of the months that followed the accident as he and his family tried to come to terms with their pain and move forward. Mr. Chapman managed to create a most phenomenal tribute to his daughter through his incredible faith.

So why two copies of the CD? Why not just one? I don't know, but I can't help but think God intended for me to end up with one of them. Steven Curtis Chapman knew nothing about me, but for some reason, he handed Katy two CDs who, in turn, sent one of them home to her mom who, in turn, gave it to me. When I first listened to it, I could not believe the strength he must have had to summon in order to cut through such raw pain and emotion—pain and emotion, coincidentally, that mirrored my own. Any attempts that I could make to convey what this music has come to mean to me would indeed be paltry.

The Saturday before Christmas, our first Christmas without Gavin, I had a car accident, my first since I was seventeen. While I obviously don't view the accident itself as a gift from God, I do know so many of the circumstances of that day were under His control. First and foremost on my mind immediately after the crash was, *Thank God Rhys isn't with me!*

She was supposed to go with me that snowy morning to my mom's house, about thirty minutes away. However, when she woke up and saw the record-setting snowfall on the ground, she figured she better take advantage of it because, "It won't last forever, ya know."

Not that we live in northeast Ohio. If there's anything we can count on in winter, it's plenty of snow. Grandma would have to wait nonetheless.

I realized the second of the day's gifts when I was able to get out of what was left of my car on my own power. Although I was incredibly sore, I was able to walk away from something I probably shouldn't have survived. My car was a mess, but no other property damage, no blood, no broken bones, no head injury, and no one else was hurt. Was someone watching over me that day? No doubt.

Then the oddest thought came to me. It suddenly occurred to me just how much I wanted to live. Up until that very moment, I wasn't so sure. It's not so much that I wanted to live for my own sake. I wanted to live for Rhys. Believe me, if I didn't have her, I would be ready to go any day if it means I could be with my son. But after the wreck, I understood that it would certainly never be by my own hand. I know that's another very odd statement, but I'd be lying if I said the thought never came to me in my grief.

Later on that same the day, I took my husband's car to get groceries across town. No sooner had I begun shopping when he called to tell me the dog got hit hard by a car and was coughing up blood. Mike didn't think he would make it. All the way home, I pleaded with God over and over again not to take Dingo, not so much for me or Mike, but for Rhys's sake. I begged, "Please don't do this to Rhys!" She was madly in love, as we all were, with the newest addition to the family. How would she be able to handle another loss?

By the time I got home, Mike had already brought the dog into the house, got the name and address of the closest emergency vet clinic, and had Rhys all ready to go. When I ran into the house, there was a trail of blood drops leading up to my bedroom. I was definitely fearing the worst. My normally ADHD dog was just lying there, not moving, and gave me the saddest look when he saw me. I remember thinking, *How on earth can our family deal with this right before Christmas? How much is enough?*

We braced ourselves for the inevitable in the waiting room. As it turned out, the worst thing about that vet visit was the bill. Dingo was fine! The vet couldn't find anything wrong with him and felt the blood he was coughing up was due to the impact and would subside. She sent us home with pain medication (for me or the dog?), and that was that. By the next night, he was chasing the cats through the house like nothing had happened. Based on Mike's description of the impact, which he and Rhys both witnessed, Dingo should have been dead instantly.

Our family dodged two major bullets that day. How could I possibly not have felt that God was watching over us? There simply is no other explanation. Pure luck? Coincidence? If I had any lingering doubts about God's existence prior to that day, they were completely obliterated in the few precious seconds that it took for my car to come to rest. At the end of that incredible day, I had another amazing revelation: how on earth could I have been mad at God all those years while at the same time professing not to believe in Him? How was it possible for me to be mad at someone who supposedly didn't exist?

Unfortunately, the following spring, Dingo finally met his match. We got a late winter blast, and the ground was completely whited out. Dingo was also completely white. He crossed the zapping barrier and was out roaming the street, and one of our neighbors didn't see him in all the white. He did not get a reprieve that time. I had to have a very difficult conversation with Rhys that day on our way home from school. She took it pretty hard at first. I told her that since Gavin couldn't have a dog while he was alive because of his allergies, God gave him Dingo to have in heaven. That seemed to work because a few hours later, she asked when we could go get another dog.

Over the last several years of my career prior to Gavin's death, I had been feeling the itch to do something different. I wanted to stay in education, and I wanted to stay at my current school, but I had desperately needed a change, more so after he died. I had been teaching five different subjects each day at the high school for eighteen years. Opportunities to move into another area came and went, and I always wanted to kick myself for not having the courage to pursue any of them.

Eventually, this old dog went back to school and got an endorsement to my current master's degree. When I finished, I was certified in educational technology. My goal was to replace a teacher who would be retiring soon; alas, he decided to stay for five more years. Okay, now what was I going to do? When an eighth grade language arts teacher announced her retirement, I saw yet another opportunity to change. Instead, I found myself in the middle of a career dilemma. I had myself so worked up over what to do that I couldn't sleep, and I was just a hot mess. I made that mole hill into Mt. Everest. The conflict was augmented when I heard our librarian would be retiring in another year. *Should I get out now and go down to the junior high even though I didn't really want to? Was I that desperate for something different? That would have been a very drastic change for me. Or should I just bide my time for one more year in the classroom and then move to the library position?*

I had visions of the little angel and little devil each seated on a shoulder, tugging at me in both directions. This conflict was making more of a mess of me than I usually was. On top of wanting a change, if I didn't make a move soon, I would have to have all of Gavin's friends as students shortly. I don't think I could have handled having them all without him there. It was tough enough being in the same school let alone being their teacher. What to do? what to do...

It finally dawned on me that I should run it by God. I had certainly run it past everyone else for their input. I asked Him to help me see things more clearly, help me make the right move. I truly agonized over my direction at that point. After a few days of both agony and prayer, the whole mess just seemed so clear to me all of a sudden. I've *never* wanted to teach junior high. What was I thinking! I could sit tight for one more year. Compared to all the other adverse situations I had faced, this was nothing. I can't believe how much better I felt as once again, the weight of a dilemma was lifted from me through prayer.

Even now, I am in awe of this new perspective I have on the power of prayer. I never held much stock in it before. I asked Him to save the dog for Rhys's sake, and He came through. I asked Him to guide me, and He answered. I was never before so open and attune to receiving His gifts. What an incredible feeling!

Perhaps the greatest of all of God's gifts to me has been the gift of friendship. Not only does adversity test our character, but it also most certainly puts friendship to the test. Those who are still standing firm when the dust settles are shining examples of true friends. Some have been standing beside me for eons, and some have just recently entered my life. Regardless of their seniority, they have saved me in one way or another.

My husband is, without a doubt, my best friend. On most days, I would rather spend time with him than anyone else. Not every married person can say that about his/her spouse. If you were to ask my husband who his best friend is, I know without question he would say it's me. Not only do we love each other, but we also actually *like* each other. There's a big difference, and the two don't always go hand in hand. Sure, we have our moments like all married people, but at the end of the day, we know who we are and we have each other's backs. Mike has saved me from myself so many times that I have lost count. He is a wonderful husband, a fabulous father, an engaging teacher and coach, and simply a good man. I truly don't know where I would be without him.

The biggest test of our friendship came with the death of our son. I'm sure if I was to look at divorce statistics following the death of a child, they wouldn't be very encouraging. But we were determined to hang on to each other and preserve our family. If you have never experienced the loss of a child, you cannot possibly imagine the strain it puts on all of your relationships, not just a marriage. While others moved on, we were caught in slow motion, just trying to figure out how to get up each day.

Contrary to what some think, grief isn't a stage that we go through and then come out the other side all healed. It's an ever-evolving state that we slip in and out of, sometimes just dipping a toe and other times diving in feet first. Mike and I each continue to grieve in our own way, and there have been times when it was extremely difficult to lend support to each other. But the knowledge that we are ultimately in this together has helped us constantly renew our commitment to our family. We have made it through this because we *wanted* to make it through.

My friend Kathy and I have been friends since the fifth grade. We have certainly had our ups and downs over the years, especially the teen years. We have seen and done it all together, and we know the best and worst about each other. She is my go-to girl, especially when the stuff is hitting the fan. Nobody knows me like she does. And even though her life has certainly not been a cake walk, I have always been able to count on her without question.

When I came home from the hospital from having a double mastectomy, I could hardly move. I never realized how much we use our pectoral muscles until I was missing about a third of mine. Kathy was there. She helped me shower, do my hair, and whatever else I needed. She never once blinked an eye when she saw what was left of my chest and all of the drainage tubes and stitches. The night my son died, Kathy was the first person I called after I told my parents. The next day, she was one of the first at my house to help manage the total chaos. And that's just the tip of the iceberg.

My friendship with Andrea happened by accident. Or did it? So many events led to it that I can only assume God put us together because He knew how much I was going to need her. If we hadn't moved our kids to this school, if Andrea hadn't offered riding lessons for Gavin, if I hadn't decided to ride as well, if Gavin hadn't died. If, if, if. So many *ifs* don't simply add up to coincidence. She was placed in my life for a reason. More than anyone or anything else, she is the one who has ultimately helped me find my way back to God. Her unwavering faith in His love has forced me to examine myself in ways that I have ignored for over thirty years. I don't always like what I find, but I have learned to ask Him to help me change those parts of myself.

Andrea realizes that I am a work in progress, and she accepts me without prejudice. When I ask her a question about God and she can't give me an answer, she says, "I'll get back to you on that," and she always does. She and her horses literally saved me from slipping into a very dark place. And she continues to minister my ever-grieving heart to this day. This can't be an easy job for her as it is a constant one. Just when I think I'm doing well, I stumble once again, and she and my other friends are there to grab hold of me and set me upright.

In my greatest time of need, Nancy is another friend who came through for me in big ways. And like Kathy and Andrea, she continues to guide me through some of my darkest moments. While others have moved on, she has remained steadfast in understanding that my grieving is far from over. Don't get me wrong—I don't blame others for moving on. That is the very nature of life: it does indeed move on. Mine just goes on in a different way now. As with Andrea, Nancy serves as my spiritual docent and is genuinely interested in helping me find my way. Her steadfast faith and commitment to God is inspiring, and the measures she takes to tend to me are incredibly comforting.

Let me share with you one of my favorite examples of the lengths she goes to. A few months after Gavin died, we ran into each other one rainy day at the grocery store as I was coming in, and she was checking out. Her cart was overflowing with bags as I stopped to say hello. There was no time for chit-chat as there was quite a line behind her, so I went on my way through the store. Many minutes later, I turned the corner and there she was. After loading up all her bags into her car while it was raining, she turned right back around, came back into the store to find me. All because she felt that's what a friend should do. She just wanted to know how I had been doing. How many of us would do such a thing? I'm ashamed to say it, but I'm not sure that I would have. That seemingly small gesture continues with me to this day. To me, it was huge, and there is such a lesson in it.

My friend Jenny and I didn't really know each other all that well prior to Gavin's death. The day after his funeral, we took Rhys to our county fair just to get her mind off of the week from hell that we had all been through. We saw many people that we knew that day. Some looked at us like we had no business being out in public so soon and others greeted us but clearly did not want to engage in conversation with us. I'm sure that was more out of awkwardness rather than a lack of compassion. But it was really hard for us to take that step toward our new normal, and when literally no one could give us the time of day, it hurt. Jenny saw us and did not hesitate to strike up a conversation and invite us to hang out with her family. She's been one of my best friends since then.

Then there's JD, Jenny's son. JD is a gift from God that I never could have expected. He was one of Gavin's friends who has become an incredibly important part of my life as well as Rhys's. He took Gavin's death really hard and to this day is one of the most stalwart keepers of his memory. He and I became very close once he got to high school as he spent four years' worth of study halls in my office, sometimes getting help with English and sometimes just talking about nothing all that important. I used to tease him about making sure they spelled my name correctly on his diploma. He has become an excellent surrogate big brother to Rhys and is a crucial member of our family. I love him as one of my own. He will never know just how much he has helped Rhys and me, and I know that Gavin would be so very proud of him. Initially, Jenny referred to him as my stepson, but that seemed to cause too much confusion, so I started calling him my godson. After all, he is most definitely a gift from God, and he is like a son to me, so why not?

God has seen fit to place these people and so many others (Sally, Karrie, and so many more) in my life for one reason or another. And through this, I have learned what friendship really is:

1. Being a true friend requires a great deal of work and risk; it's not easy by any means. I sometimes have to put aside my own problems and concerns to help a friend. It's risky putting my faith and trust in another human being. But I must do so without expecting anything in return.

2. I know that my friends and I won't always agree on everything, but that's okay. Through mutual respect, we can find a way to agree to disagree. Sometimes it's our differences that bind us together.

3. Most importantly, I have learned not to take true friends for granted. They are most assuredly a gift from God.

It's uncanny sometimes how timing truly is everything. This last gift from God might as well have been on a marquee lit up by a thousand lights. My family had a typical routine on Sunday mornings. My husband went to early church at 8:30, and while he was gone, I would get Rhys ready for Sunday school at 9:30. After I dropped her off, I would usually go to the grocery store then go back and pick her up at 10:30. One particular Sunday, Mike called to tell me not to rush, that Rhys was asked to stay for the second service and serve as an acolyte. I immediately had visions of that grand old church engulfed in flames. You see, my darling little angel was somewhat of a bull in a china shop. I affectionately call her my delicate little flower. She has always been such a tomboy and used to be somewhat oblivious to danger. We avoided allowing her to handle fire at all costs. To allow her to walk from the back part of the church through a section of people in chairs, up around the corner and down between rows of pews with an open flame, regardless of how small, was, in my opinion, just asking for trouble.

I thought I should go get her a little early just in case they needed help evacuating anyone from the church. You can only imagine my relief when I pulled up to the church and did not see one wisp of smoke. Whew! Rather than wait in the car, as I normally did, I decided to go in to make sure she hadn't tied everyone up. On entering, I heard the minister still delivering his message, so I waited down the steps in the foyer and listened.

On this particular day, Pastor George was talking about doubt, of all things, and how it's okay to experience doubt, even long periods of doubt. He said that even the most faithful at times experience their moments of doubt. It's okay; God understands. The minister went on to say that as long as we come back to God, that's what's important. We need to ask Him for guidance and deliverance. I felt as though he was speaking directly to me! I found myself standing there with tears streaming down my face as I sobbed uncontrollably. How did the minister know? He couldn't have possibly known that I would walk in at that moment to hear his reassuring words. No, he couldn't have, but God did. I feel certain that it was His guiding hand that prompted me to go in that day rather than wait in the car. As I stood there trying to collect myself, a woman whom I had never met before, came by, put her hand gently on my arm, and said, "It will be okay. You'll figure it out. Trust Him," and walked away.

I challenge anyone to tell me that the events of that morning were mere coincidences. I will feel the power of those few precious moments for the rest of my life.

I have learned to be very selective about with whom I share my "signs from Gavin" and my "gifts from God." When I do tell people about them, the reactions are mixed. Some look at me like I have totally lost it; there are a few who simply chalk it up to my grief and wishful thinking. However, there are several who literally get goosebumps because they have had similar experiences. These few people are usually so relieved to hear someone else's stories because they were afraid to share their own.

I ask both God and Gavin daily for signs. I desperately need constant reminders that they are with me. But I tell them I'm not always the most observant person, so they shouldn't be subtle. I tell

God He needs to put his message in bright neon with arrows point-ing to it saying, "Hey, Denise. It's me, God." So many of God's gifts are like foreshadows in literature: you might not really know that the author is using foreshadow until you reach the relevant part of the story where it all connects. And so it sometimes is with God. We might not interpret something as a sign from Him until we get to another part of our lives where it suddenly makes sense. He gives us all gifts. We just have to be brave enough and open to receiving them. So through some of His gifts, His persistent love, and patience with me, I have learned to sit back and keep "reading." I now have enough faith and trust to understand that it all will be revealed eventually.

> *Trust in the Lord with all your heart and lean not on your own understanding; in all your ways sub-mit to him, and he will make your paths straight.*[5]
> —Proverbs 3:5–6

Chapter 7

Where I Am Now

I was always skeptical of those who claimed to have heard directly from God. Not only was I skeptical, but I was envious as well. I wished so badly that He would speak to me and tell me what I was supposed to do, how I was supposed to go on. I begged Him to reveal my purpose to me. Nothing. For the longest time, nothing. Then I got my wish.

I have only shared what I'm about to tell you with a handful of people. I'm not sure why exactly, but I'd be willing to guess it has something to do with the skepticism and jealousy I mentioned above: (1) I knew most people wouldn't believe me, and (2) if they did believe me, I wasn't prepared to share such a personal experience with just anyone. This is by far the hardest part of this book to write for that reason. Even as I sit here writing this, I struggle to come up with an adequate description of what happened next that will come close to doing it justice.

It was about 6:00 a.m. on a summer Saturday as I was driving away from the local convenience store where I got my requisite morning diet soda to which I was highly addicted at the time. I was heading to the farm in Canfield where I boarded my horse to load up for a day of showing. Shortly after Gavin's death, I developed the habit of talking aloud to God while I am driving alone. I don't know that I would call it praying per se; most times it's a full-blown conversation, albeit one-sided. As I pulled through a green light that morning, I said very simply out loud, "Lord, I don't know you very well, but I'd like to."

Immediately, my entire body filled up with a sensation such as I had never felt before. It started on the inside, right in my core, and absolutely flooded me with an inexplicable warmth and peace. I literally thought I was having a health issue or something and looked to see where I could pull off the road. But it happened so fast that I barely had time to pick a spot before it was over. So fast yet it seemed that for that brief moment, time had stopped so that I could fully appreciate what was happening to me. I felt like I had been turned inside out with every part of my being exposed. No thunderbolts appeared, no flashing lights, no parting of the skies; no words were spoken, yet I knew in no uncertain terms that God was saying to me, "You are mine."

It was, without a doubt, the most incredibly spiritual experience of my life. Talk about a defining moment! I wish so much that I had the ability to convey in words just how prodigious it was or how profoundly it affected me. I was left quite astonished and couldn't wait to get to the horse show to share it with my friend Andrea. Of all people, I knew she would believe me, and she would understand just how amazing those few precious seconds were. When I finally found a few private minutes with her, I laid bare my soul. The magnitude of what had happened that morning swept over me like a hurricane, and I was sobbing so hard, I could barely make myself understood to her.

That moment completely obliterated any lingering doubts that I had of God's existence and His love for me. Of all the people in this world, He chose *me* to share that moment with. I don't know why He felt I was worthy of it at that particular time, but it is the most precious gift I have ever received. I told a few select others about my experience, and true to what I predicted, the reactions were mixed. I had to assure one or two that, no, I didn't have gas, or no, I hadn't been drinking. Seriously! It was only 6:00 in the morning! But there were a few who totally got it. Ironically, for someone who usually has an insatiable need for validation, I didn't feel that need this time. I knew what I felt, I knew where it came from, and I got the only validation I needed, from God. I don't really care what anyone else thinks of it.

So where did that experience leave me? Well, that's an interesting question, and the answer might vary from day to day. I gave the Lord an open invitation into my heart and life, and He RSVP'd loud and clear. He basically let me know that the ball is in my court and has been pretty much my entire life. While my faith and trust in Him are on solid ground, I still have other issues that need to be worked out. It's all a little overwhelming. It's not like I've *never* known Him, but I've been away from Him for so long; now that I have come back to Him, I want to take one step at a time so that I can be a fully participating partner in this relationship. I have accepted that I am a constant work in progress.

I struggle to refer to myself as a Christian mostly because I have a hard time coming to grips with the concept of the Trinity. When I was growing up, I accepted what I was taught without question, and I was taught that God was God but in three persons. Okay, think about that for a minute, especially from a child's perspective: the Father, the Son, and the Holy Spirit aren't different parts of God; they're three persons that exist in one being as the same entity and can't be separated from each other. That's pretty deep stuff even for adults. So as I child, I kept it simple and accepted that I was a Christian, and that's that. But now, that's not enough. It's not enough to simply declare myself a Christian without knowing what all that entails. So until I come to an understanding of what it means to call myself a Christian, I am uncomfortable doing so.

Many of the issues that I feel I need to deal with seem to center around organized religion. It seems that so much of what I believe in conflicts with other Christians' beliefs and with some doctrines. First and foremost, I refuse to believe in a wrathful and vengeful God. My God is forgiving but stern, wise, warm, loving, and patient. I am a perfect example of those qualities. When I turned my back on Him, He did not forget about me. He always kept His eye on me, and when I was making all the wrong choices for myself, He kept me from serious harm or from seriously harming others. Don't get me wrong—He let me learn from my mistakes, sometimes the hard way. But looking back now, I can't believe some of the incredibly stupid choices I made and came out relatively unscathed in the end. Most importantly, He forgave me and warmly welcomed me back.

One of the things about my beliefs that tends to bother my Christian relatives and friends is that I don't believe in a literal interpretation of the Bible (not that I am overly familiar with it, mind you). When I was a high school English teacher, critical analysis was the backbone of our literature studies; I asked my students to analyze, evaluate, question, and assess everything they read. Looking at the Bible analytically, I personally find too many incongruities. For example, I battle with the notion that the entire human race came from two people. By the third generation, inbreeding would start to take its genetic toll. To me, taking the Bible literally is like thinking George Orwell's *Animal Farm* is just about a bunch of talking animals who take over a farm or that *The Crucible* (Arthur Miller) is really about witches.

Please don't get me wrong. I am certainly not comparing what lies within the Bible to other pieces of literature. I'm not saying that the stories aren't true or that there aren't valuable lessons. What I am saying is that I grapple with some of the concepts and tend to look for the symbolism in the Bible stories versus a literal interpretation.

I also refuse to accept the idea that God takes attendance each Sunday in the millions of churches around the world. Why do others feel that the only way to be a good Christian is to be in church each week? Therefore, those who aren't there must be *bad* Christians? Why do some Christian churches have way different rules than others? Why does the church secretary type up a prayer in the weekly bulletin that we all must say together? Why are some religions incredibly more ritualistic than others? These are just a few of the things that bother me. When I look into certain origins, it seems to me to get pretty political. I wish there were simple answers, but there are not. I certainly do not mean to insult anyone who thinks differently than I do. I realize that many find comfort and purpose in some of the things with which I take issue. I think, in the end, the key is to find what works best for us individually.

Perhaps the concept that causes me the most angst is hypocrisy. As I look back on my mini defining moments, at the root of them all is the underlying theme of hypocrisy. I might not have known what that word meant back then, but I certainly was able to recognize it in those particular situations. But what I have always been so readily willing to see in others, I was unwilling to see in myself. The reconnection I have found with God has caused me to do much reflection of my own actions and thoughts. Much to my shock and dismay, I have discovered that I am as a big a hypocrite as anyone else I have ever met! I think we are all hypocritical at times; that's the nature of the beast. As natural as it may be, when we let our hypocrisy affect not only our earthly relationships but also our relationship with God, we need to seriously check ourselves.

Because of conflicts with organized religion, I don't consider myself religious. I'm spiritual. I believe in God. I believe in heaven. I don't hold to one doctrine over another, nor do I live my life based on the principles of this church or that one. I go to church when I feel like I need to or when I simply want to hear an uplifting message from the pastor (who is a fantastic storyteller, by the way), but I don't go out of some sense of obligation or to please anyone else. I live my life trying to do what's right. I try to be kind to others, and I try to offer help when and where it's needed. Sometimes I'm Johnny on the spot, and sometimes I miss the mark completely, but I keep trying.

> *We've all got both light and dark inside us. What matters is the part we choose to act on. That's who we really are.*
> —Sirius Black from *Harry Potter and the Order of the Phoenix*[6]

Chapter 8

A Work in Progress

One of the most priceless revelations for me has been that of the value of family and friends. Not that I didn't value family and friends before, but with the death of my son came a renewed appreciation for just how lucky I am. It is so true that many of us take the people in our lives for granted. Once in a while, we need to be reminded of all they do for us. Unfortunately, I learned that lesson the hard way. One minute my son was hugging me goodbye as he left for football practice, the next he was gone. I blinked, and life as I knew it was over. The regrets I have to carry with me the rest of my days are incredibly painful.

Be that as it may, perhaps the biggest realization I have come to on this journey is that we are not guaranteed anything in this life. God owes us nothing. It is we who owe Him, and if we receive any intervention, it's at His discretion. We are given this life to see what we can do with it, to see how worthy we are of the next one.

We are left to our own devices here. Yes, God can intervene if that's His plan and will, but He's not obligated to do so. It's up to us to get through the best we can. Do we dare ask him for help and guidance? Of course we do! It's when we expect it and demand it that we set ourselves up for huge letdowns. All we can do while we are here is survive, sometimes thrive, and help each other do the same. We must learn to trust in Him, lean on Him, and most importantly, talk with Him, for it is through prayer that the healing comes.

I have realized that there is no way possible for any one of us to have all of the answers. We simply aren't meant to. That's for another place and time. And if any think that they do have it all figured out, they are in way worse shape than I am. It bothers me that there are those who seem to have an answer or counterpoint to every question or criticism directed at them in regard to their faith. They haven't learned that there are times when it's perfectly okay to simply say, "I don't know." To me, that's the very definition of faith. We don't know, yet we still believe in Him; we still trust Him.

I have sadly become all too cognizant that life has a cruel way of knocking us down and placing obstacles in our paths. Some experience more tragedy than others while some seem to go through life with little to no adversity whatsoever. Do those of us who suffer more appreciate what we do have any more than those who don't suffer? I don't know, but I sure would like to try the other side of the coin for a while. I do, nonetheless, think that when bad things happen to us, we are presented with golden opportunities to rise up and test our strength and our faith. Unfortunately, that's a little easier said than done. A friend once told me that God only gives us what we can handle, and some can handle more than others. What I used to wonder was, why did He seem to expect so much from me? I demanded to know what made Him think I could handle the ultimate challenge facing me at the time—the loss of my son. Yet here I am. Imagine that.

Up to this point, I have been able to eventually rise up after being knocked down. When I was diagnosed with cancer, I wasn't so sure I could rebound. But somehow, I came to recognize that I was stronger than I thought and I could indeed make it through. Did God give my grandma cancer? I can't begin to believe that, but I do know that He must have known what I would later face and helped me to appreciate her example from which to draw strength and inspiration.

But His latest test of my ability to rise above almost proved too much for me. For the longest time after Gavin's death, I just didn't want to be here on this earth. In fact, if it was not for my daughter, I'm not so sure that I would still be here. She has given me a purpose that reaches far beyond typical maternal feelings. Here I am, many years after Gavin's death, and each day continues to be somewhat of a struggle. There are days when I let the sorrow grab hold of me, and I am flooded with sadness. All I can do at this point is surrender to His will and trust Him to lift me and my family up. And you can bet that I constantly ask Him to stop testing me so much. I think I should be exempt for a long while!

A couple of years after we lost Gavin, my husband ran into a friend of his who asked how we were getting along. This always proves to be a difficult response for either of us. Do they really want to know how we are getting along, or are they simply inquiring because they think it's the right thing to ask? Either way, they should be prepared for replies that could possibly run the gamut. Most days, we are okay; there are even many days that we are better than okay. But there are also days that drown us in utter anguish even to this day. I think about my son *every* day. I miss him *every* day. It *never* goes away.

This same friend emailed an incredible metaphoric story to Mike that perfectly relates our status. The original story was posted as a response on Reddit to another member who wrote the following: "My friend just died. I don't know what to do." The user GSnows posted this eloquent response:

> Alright, here goes. I'm old. What that means is that I've survived (so far) and a lot of people I've known and loved did not. I've lost friends, best friends, acquaintances, co-workers, grandparents, mom, relatives, teachers, mentors, students, neighbors, and a host of other folks. I have no children, and I can't imagine the pain it must be to lose a child. But here's my two cents.
>
> I wish I could say you get used to people dying. I never did. I don't want to. It tears a hole through me whenever somebody I love dies, no matter the circumstances. But I don't want it to "not matter." I don't want it to be something that just passes. My scars are a testament to the love and the relationship that I had for and with that person. And if the scar is deep, so was the love.

So be it. Scars are a testament to life. Scars are a testament that I can love deeply and live deeply and be cut, or even gouged, and that I can heal and continue to live and continue to love. And the scar tissue is stronger than the original flesh ever was. Scars are a testament to life. Scars are only ugly to people who can't see.

As for grief, you'll find it comes in waves. When the ship is first wrecked, you're drowning, with wreckage all around you. Everything floating around you reminds you of the beauty and the magnificence of the ship that was, and is no more. And all you can do is float. You find some piece of the wreckage and you hang on for a while. Maybe it's some physical thing. Maybe it's a happy memory or a photograph. Maybe it's a person who is also floating. For a while, all you can do is float. Stay alive.

In the beginning, the waves are 100 feet tall and crash over you without mercy. They come 10 seconds apart and don't even give you time to catch your breath. All you can do is hang on and float. After a while, maybe weeks, maybe months, you'll find the waves are still 100 feet tall, but they come further apart. When they come, they still crash all over you and wipe you out.

But in between, you can breathe, you can function. You never know what's going to trigger the grief. It might be a song, a picture, a street intersection, the smell of a cup of coffee. It can be just about anything... and the wave comes crashing. But in between waves, there is life.

Somewhere down the line, and it's different for everybody, you find that the waves are only 80 feet tall. Or 50 feet tall. And while they still come, they come further apart. You can see them coming.

An anniversary, a birthday, or Christmas, or landing at O'Hare. You can see it coming, for the most part, and prepare yourself.

And when it washes over you, you know that somehow you will, again, come out the other side. Soaking wet, sputtering, still hanging on to some tiny piece of the wreckage, but you'll come out.

Take it from an old guy. The waves never stop coming, and somehow you don't really want them to. But you learn that you'll survive them. And other waves will come. And you'll survive them too. If you're lucky, you'll have lots of scars from lots of loves. And lots of shipwrecks.[7]

This amazing, beautifully said post sums us up perfectly. The difference between then and now is that I am learning how to hang on to the Lord when those waves do hit.

Through my son's death though, I have come to understand that it is okay to be angry with God; it's okay to question Him. It's a relationship. Why should our relationship with Him be any different than our other personal relationships? It must be mutual, however. We owe Him the same trust, honesty, loyalty, and unconditional love that we give to our spouses, children, and others in our lives. Do we get angry or question them? Of course we do. Do we forgive, compromise, patch up, and move on with them? You bet. And so it must be with God. Who understands human nature better than the one who created us? So naturally, He understands our anger and our questions as well.

I have a sneaky suspicion that I am just in the infancy of my quest. I have already learned so much about myself in these years after my son's death because of my need for something else in my life, but I also know that I have a long journey still ahead of me. And although I would do anything to have Gavin with me again, I truly appreciate the awakening that came after his death. What a shame it would have been if I had not learned from the most tragic event in my life. A situation that might have caused others to walk away from God and give up altogether has ultimately brought me back to Him.

The realizations I have come to are somewhat random, but they have come through a lot of agony, questioning, and searching. It is important to note that I did not directly seek Him. I silently wished for answers, but not necessarily from Him. At least not initially. I feel as though God purposely pursued me. He became a comforting shadow that stood beside me, letting me know that I was welcome back any time. He didn't push, tug, or coerce. He just waited by me patiently and bided His time until I was ready.

I truly believe that He is set on a mission to gently guide me toward a specific purpose, I just can't figure out what it is. I have trouble putting this feeling into words, but since Gavin's death, I have felt as though God has been clearing not just one but several paths for me from which I can choose for myself with His guidance, of course. Sometimes, I keep coming back to a crossroads. My instinct right now is to just keep moving straight ahead. Regardless of which path I end up taking, I believe it will ultimately lead to Him. So I know what my final destination is. I just have to decide what to do between now and then.

I recognize that we all must find our own way on our journeys to discover who we are spiritually. Some of us take the long way around while others take a more direct route. Each of our journeys is influenced by a host of elements, some within our control, others not so much, some of them helpful influences, others destructive. It's important for us all to remember that there are no right or wrong paths, just different ones. Where we each end up is the point of it all.

While I was trying to finish up writing this book, I was really stumped by how to end it. As a former English teacher, I felt an insatiable need to write a solid climactic conclusion to wrap up my story, which would reveal some amazing epiphany and inspire its readers. But then I realized that my adventure isn't over by any means; hopefully I'm not even close to being at the end of it. Therefore, how could I finish my story? The best I can do is to leave you with this:

I know that I am a sinner, most days a really big one. Each morning I ask the Lord to help me be a better person than I was the day before. And each day I sin again. Multiple times. I catch myself occasionally, but many times I go unchecked. So I vow to try harder tomorrow. And when tomorrow comes, I ask Him to help me to be better than I was the day before once again. And so on. As humans, we are never going to be perfect. However, that doesn't give us the excuse to behave how we want. The point is to try for perfection, try to be better in the eyes of God. I'm willing to bet the effort goes a long way. We must try to be the best version of ourselves every single day.

> *Remember how far you've come, not just how far*
> *you have to go. You are not where you want to*
> *be, but neither are you where you used to be.*
> —Rick Warren[8]

Epilogue

As purposeless as I feel at times, my hope is that some reading this little book will examine the defining moments in their own lives and come to realizations of their own. So much of my healing began when I quit trying to wrestle the control away from God and to put my faith in Him. By putting my faith in Him and trusting Him completely, such an enormous weight has been lifted from me. We all live by faith in one form or another, no matter how small the details are. When I get up in the middle of the night, I have faith that someone hasn't rearranged the furniture so that I don't trip. In the morning, I have faith that my daughter will get up on her own on time to get to school. On my way to work, I have faith that the other drivers coming toward me will stay in their lane. I have faith that I will finally get all of my answers. I have faith that I will have my son in my arms once again. I have faith that one day I will stand in front of my Lord and be warmly welcomed home with Him. Until then, I have much to do. God is not done with me yet.

We are not given a good life or a bad life. We are given a life. It's up to us to make it good or bad.
—Ward Foley[9]

Notes

1   Ron Shelton, dir., *Tin Cup* (U.S.: Warner Bros., 1996), DVD.
2   *Merriam-Webster Dictionary*, 2018, https://www.merriam-webster.com/ dictionary/ agnostic?utm_campaign=sd&utm_ medium=serp&utm_source=jsonld.
3   C. S Lewis, *Surprised by Joy* (San Diego, CA: Harcourt Brace and World, 1955), pp. 227.
4   Allison DuBois, *We Are Their Heaven: Why the Dead Never Leave Us* (New York, NY: Simon & Schuster, 2006).
5   Proverbs 3, *The Holy Bible* (New International Version, NIV), Biblica. 2018. www.biblica.com/bible/niv/proverbs/3/.
6   David Yates, dir., *Harry Potter and the Order of the Phoenix* (U.S.: Warner Bros., 2007), DVD.
7   "Redditt Assistance,". 2018, https://www.reddit.com/r/Assistance/comments/ hax0t/my_ friend_just_died_i_dont_know_what_to_do/c1u0rx2/.
8   Rick Warren, *The Purpose Driven Life: What on Earth Am I Here For?* (Expanded ed., Grand Rapids, MI: Zondervan, 2012), pp. 220–221.
9   Ward Foley, *Scarman*, https://www.wardfoley.com/.

My husband was already bald, so when I lost
my hair after chemo started, we decided to have
some fun with it and get our portrait done.

This is one of my favorite pictures of Rhys and Gavin together:
one of the rare moments when they weren't picking at each other.

This was taken at Barefoot Landing at Myrtle
Beach about 6 weeks before Gavin died. It was
the best family vacation we had ever taken.

This was also taken while at Myrtle Beach. He was a
different kid when he was on a horse; so relaxed and
confident. He always connected to all sorts of animals.

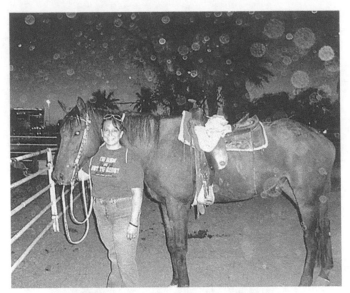

My guide took this of me after my desert trail ride.
Afterward was when I learned about the orbs.

I was asked by the chief radiologist at Salem
Community Hospital to do a photo shoot for ads he
planned to run for their mammography unit.
photo credit: Endia Wisser Photography

JD has become an integral part of our family and has been an excellent big brother to Rhys.

When Rhys turned 16, we allowed her to get a tattoo in memory of her brother.

About the Author

photo credit: Jada Landgraver Photography

Denise, a graduate of Kent State University and Walsh University, lives with her husband and daughter in Salem, Ohio. For twenty years, she taught Spanish and English before becoming the librarian/literacy coach at a small rural high school. She spent the majority of her adult life questioning God's existence until the death of her son forced her to examine the defining moments in her life. Through God's love and patience, she is learning to lean on Him as she begins to heal.

CPSIA information can be obtained
at www.ICGtesting.com
Printed in the USA
LVHW030355070519
616790LV00002B/259/P

9 781644 588277